Dancers at Sea
& Other Tales

by

The Horton Writing Group

This paperback first published in 2003 by
Inklemaker
Tremymor, Port Eynon, Swansea SA3 1NL

© Summer 2003 listed contributors of
The Horton Writing Group
© Cover Illustration by Frank Thomas

ISBN 0-9546271-0-5

Foreword

For the first time, the Horton Writing Group offers a collection of stories, essays and poems for your enjoyment.

Selected to entertain the reader, these writings illustrate our contrasting styles and varied experiences. Where two or more items share a title, they show how different members of the group respond, each in his/her own way, to a creative challenge.

The group members are:

Barbara Griffiths	Mike Roberts
David Griffiths	Pam El-Hosaini
Frank Thomas	Reni Stableforth
Linda Dobbs	Tarrick El-Hosaini
Margaret Rees	Vernon Griffiths

Summer 2003

CONTENTS

Vernon Griffiths

DANCERS AT SEA

Rupert and Beatrice Dancer prided themselves on being something out of the ordinary. Barely two years of marriage had consolidated not only their relationship but also their confidence in each other. Each one complemented the other to such an extent that they usually thought as one – and this was vital in the work that they undertook together.

Their joint occupation, as far as organisations such as the Inland Revenue were concerned, was 'Private Detectives'.

Now, for such a sophisticated couple, one would have expected a somewhat more glamorous title, but if 'Private Detectives' was good enough for old-time film stars William Powell and Myrna Loy, then it was perfectly acceptable for the Dancers . . . certainly much better than 'Dancers Incorporated'.

You see, Rupert and Beatrice looked upon William Powell and Myrna Loy as their role models. For those of you who are unfamiliar with the names, perhaps a word of explanation might help. William Powell and Myrna Loy were Hollywood stars when the world was black and white. Between them, they churned out film upon film in which they solved case upon case . . . fraud, theft and murder . . . anything and everything that the fiendish criminal mind could perpetrate on an unsuspecting society. Powell was known as the 'Thin Man'. His wife was just his wife. But, together they were a formidable pair – criminologists at the top of their form. For cinema screen purposes only, of course.

Whenever problems arose, Rupert and Beatrice would dig deep into their video archives and play yet another episode of the 'Thin Man'. The films were so well scripted that countless crimes were solved even before they were committed – well that was the way it seemed. What was good enough for Hollywood was good enough for the Dancers. You could not do better than that, and it was on this basis that Rupert and Beatrice built up a reputation, which even William Powell and Myrna Loy would have envied.

Then, a distressing and baffling incident occurred. The Dancers' home was broken into. No jewellery was stolen, the few valuable paintings were undisturbed, and even the state-of-the-art television sets and sound equipment had obviously not merited the attention of the thief – or was it thieves? It was totally mystifying, even for the highly experienced Dancers.

Rupert and Beatrice were so distressed that they neglected William and Myrna. So often in the past, at moments such as this, they had digested all the various strands of 'Thin Man' rationale and logic and it had really paid dividends. But now, for no clear reason, William and Myrna had not been consulted. The Dancers were unable to think coherently. They could not believe that somebody would even dare to break into their home.

Many hours later, Rupert sighed deeply. "I feel as if we have been cast adrift in a rudderless dinghy in the middle of the biggest ocean in the world. How can we explain this to our clients?"

"For a start, we will not report the break-in to the police." Beatrice was quite emphatic. "Publicity such as this will shatter people's confidence in us. Let's sit down and try to puzzle it out in the best William and Myrna style."

Rupert turned towards the video cupboard. "Strange that we should forget all about them at a time like this." He slid back the wooden door and reached for a couple of tapes. "My God, they've gone!"

"What?"

Rupert was frantic, pointlessly searching through an almost empty cupboard. "Our 'Thin Man' tapes – they've gone – except one."

Beatrice, too, was stunned. "Who could have taken them? What use are they to anybody else?"

"What use indeed . . . " Rupert stared at the gaps left by the missing tapes – and suddenly something stirred inside him. In true 'Thin Man' style, things were clicking into place.

"That painter chap you had in the other day – what was his name?" he asked Beatrice.

"Surely you don't think that he had anything to do with the break-in. He did the job very well, and he left a note to say that he'd finished. I remember he signed it 'Nicholas' – no surname, but I suppose we can find out from the firm if you really want to."

Beatrice picked up the telephone directory and rustled through the pages. She was beginning to panic. There were no A1 PAINTERS listed – but that was definitely the name printed on the side of the van. She remembered it distinctly. After all, she prided herself on being able to recall the minutest of details, just like Myrna Loy. Beatrice had always admired the polished manner in which Myrna put everything into perspective up on the silver screen.

Last week, casually chatting in the local shop, Beatrice had mentioned to a friend that her kitchen needed painting. She had everything ready for doing it; it was just finding the time. Before her friend could reply, a voice behind her called out. "I'll be around in the morning about nine. I'll do the job for you." Startled, she turned around but failed to find the body that went with the voice.

The Dancers had to leave the house just before nine o'clock the following morning but Beatrice left a key with her neighbour and instructions for the painter on the front door asking for the invoice to be sent in the post. As they drove away from the house, she was reassured to see the white van pulling up outside.

Describing it all in detail to Rupert now made her realise how foolish she had been, how she had taken for granted that A1 PAINTERS were genuine. At the time, Rupert had been so preoccupied with a very awkward investigation that he had not even bothered to query the peculiar arrangements.

"We have committed the most elementary errors for a pair with our experience. I can't believe it really . . ." Rupert became lost in thought. Then, "We have often come to the conclusion, haven't we, that the solution to so many problems can be very simple indeed. Perhaps we should look to the more obvious first."

"And the obvious is?"

"A quick phone call to our friendly Inspector. No need to mention our break-in. For our own good we'll keep that out of the news. Let's just find out whether Nicholas the painter and decorator is on the books at the station."

It proved to be the quickest of calls . . . confirmation, indeed, that a young man – and one of the many names he used was Nicholas Charles – was well known to the local police, not only for painting and decorating, but for a few other trades as well. Young Nick had last been heard of serving nine months at her Majesty's pleasure and, as far as was known, was still serving it.

So, the Dancers were still at sea.

After the call there was a stricken silence between them for a while. They both had their eyes fixed on the videotape that Rupert kept turning and turning in his hands. Then, in accord, and with increasing astonishment, they stared at each other.

It was Rupert who blurted out, "Nicholas Charles! Nicholas Charles! NICK CHARLES! It can't be!"

Without a word, Beatrice grabbed the tape from her husband and jammed it into the video player. She fast-

8

forwarded the tape until the credits appeared on the screen. And there it was. They had simply needed to confirm in their minds what they knew only too well.

Myrna Loy and even the dog were listed as two of the stars – but top billing was given to William Powell in the role of NICK CHARLES – The Thin Man.

From that day on, Rupert and Beatrice Dancer, 'Private Detectives', continued to solve their cases and any mystery presented to them – but without the assistance of William Powell or Myrna Loy.

They had both been convinced that 'The Thin Man' had been trying to tell them something.

Rupert and Beatrice didn't need him anymore.

Nick Charles had taught them all he knew.

Mike Roberts

WAVES

Dancing, Dancing, Dancing,
Dancing at sea.
The ceaseless waves that dance
In the rolling endless sea.

The ceaseless waves that dance
In mornings crisp and clear,
The whispering wandering waves
Tell stories we wait to hear.

The whispering wandering waves
As they hiss on the sandy shore,
Tell of sailors in watery graves
Speak of those who are here no more.

As they hiss on the sandy shore
Just listen to tales they tell,
Of brave men in days of yore
Who were doomed in a watery hell.

Dancing in days of yore
The dancing dangerous sea,
Its partner the limestone cliffs,
Its mood a merciless spree.

Its partner the limestone cliffs
In delicate summer days,
As it gently caresses the sand
Its blanket a warm June haze.

As it gently caresses the sand
In the summer day of gentle youth,
Whispers thoughts you'll understand
In a sparkling foam of truth,

Whispers thoughts you'll understand.
Dancing waves of the ebbing sea
Wipe children's footsteps from the sand
And say you belong to me.

Linda Dobbs

DANCERS AT SEA

Dorothy Tattersall waltzed out to sea
on a luxury ocean liner,
her luggage restricted to ten pairs of shoes
and ten gowns by a fashion designer
renowned for his style, who'd once dressed Fred Astaire
and his twinkle-toed partner Miss Rogers,
but who now is confined to a seedy guest-house
cooking breakfasts for dubious lodgers.

Dorothy Tattersall waltzed on the swell
ably partnered by Ronald from Frome,
her torso encased in a tight corselette,
bum in bloomers, flannelette, bags of room
which were cosy and edged with Nottingham lace,
soft airtex, coloured flesh pink, free-flowing.
Nine pairs more she had packed overflowed one holdall;
were ideal to protect from winds blowing.

Dorothy Tattersall waltzed through the waves
attracting some admiring glances
from rich, portly gents on their annual quest
to find ladies to cherish, take chances,
who plied Dot with Pims and unlimited charm.
They saw her as alluring, coquettish,
though well-worn, with grey hair, sagging jowls and a limp,
unaware that to waltz was Dot's fetish.

Dorothy Tattersall waltzed, ship becalmed
in the Doldrums, mist on the water.
The orchestra played works by Strauss, Franz Lehar,
and some more upbeat stuff by Cole Porter
while Dot whispered the lyrics into Ron's ear,
moving closer now into Ron's clutches.
So distracted was he, that Ron tripped, broke a leg;
spent the rest of the cruise on two crutches.

Dorothy Tattersall waltzed, storms forecast,
with her gentlemen suitors in turn.
As they knew that her heart was now lost to Ron
interest slackened, passions ceased to burn . . .

. . . *(to be resolved and continued to 10 stanzas)*

David Griffiths

DANCERS AT SEA

Nelly, Chloe and Elly were the teenage daughters of Mr. and Mrs. Dancer. The three girls had enjoyed a privileged childhood in a country house nicely situated on a large estate in the West Country. As time passed the parents realised that the girls' early years of coughs, colds, sleepless nights, high temperatures, raging tempers and superb tantrums had actually been the easiest part of their daughters' upbringing. What, at the time, had seemed to be an unending nightmare of noise and disruption, in retrospect seemed to have been a relatively untroubled period of the family's life. Many parental sighs showed a deep longing for the good old days when the loving couple had at least been in charge of their offspring. It was obvious to any onlooker that the roles were now reversed. The girls ran rings around their father and mother with subtle suggestions, sharp practices and devious plans that come so easily to every teenage girl. Nature gifts some females with an abundance of this character development – and was given in overflowing measure to Nelly, Chloe and Elly. Mr. Dancer soon had very little hair left that could be pulled. Mrs. Dancer became prematurely grey and also developed a bad case of 'time-deafness'. This unusual condition meant that there were many occasions when she failed to hear anything at all, especially if it was noise emanating from her three 'angels'.

The girls had grown to be outstanding eye-turners. Their father found that wherever he went with his daughters there was always a large entourage of young men. His wealth and position in society meant that news of his family was often recorded in the gossip columns reserved for the rich and noble and, though he was pleased to read of the progress the girls were making in high society, he had a growing fear that one or more of them would, one day, be the source of a story that could bring disgrace upon the respected name of the family. Mrs. Dancer was aware of her husband's anxiety and ceaselessly instilled in the girls the need to be careful. She told them that scandal, like the neighbour's tomcat, was forever lurking around the corner ready to pounce on the unwary. Much of the modern idiom was abhorrent to her sensitive mind, but she felt the use of this particular analogy helped to support her concern for their safety and wellbeing.

From prep school to finishing school Nelly, Chloe and Elly had shown an aptitude for trouble. Working together to achieve their desired aims they quickly learnt that showing a united front of wide-eyed innocence prevented any serious punishment for their misdeeds. However, they were now on the party scene and in the public eye so more diligence was imperative if their escapades were to escape the pens of news reporters. But, as in nature spring follows winter, the fast maturing girls claimed increasing attention from handsome and desirable young men and were the hope of scoop headlines for the local columnists.

Some of their friends, the girls learned, resorted to a lady of mysterious ways when they wished to know something of their future. One questioning disbeliever commented that if Madame I. Gnosis could really foretell the future she would be trading in her Mini for a Rolls from her winnings on the 'gee-gees', and, also, she should immediately enter politics for she was just the kind of person needed by the next government.

The three sisters decided to pay a visit to Madame I. Gnosis, giving little thought to the possible consequences. Not as wary as they should have been, they filed into the spurious splendour of Madame's council house front room. After the customary hocus-pocus and payment according to the girls' class they listened to what the 'clairvoyant' had to say. The general brief outline of their future satisfied them all. They would marry suitably rich men and have suitably beautiful children and lead suitably idle lives. Nelly, Chloe and Elly felt there was nothing about these predictions to question, or disagree with. Light of heart and lighter of purse they filed out to the car and gave their customary photogenic smiles to the waiting photographer.

Pleased as punch the young reporter, clutching his camera, quickly made his way to the office. He was sure he had a scoop and that fame and fortune beckoned.

It was providential that a friend of the sisters, single but hopeful Bertram Bleddows, worked for the same newspaper. Before anything was printed it was his responsibility to cast his eyes over photographs and tittle-tattle columns that were to be the breakfast gossip snack for their readers. Horrified, Bertram saw the story about the Dancer girls. He had high hopes of escorting Nelly to a Christmas Ball but realised that all was lost should his parents learn about the girls' visit to a fortune-teller. Even if they didn't read the article themselves they were certain to hear the distressing story from others. With increasing alarm he thought of the dreadful shame and scandal there would be for Mr. and Mrs. Dancer. High society would be shocked and shaken to its foundation to learn the Dancer girls had entered a council house.

'Dancers at Séance' – this was the already drafted headline for the story. Bertram read it again and again, and thought long and hard before a solution came to mind. He was sure his plan would succeed for the benefit of the respective and respectable parents. Also, Nelly would be honour bound to accept his honourable attentions when she learned of his protective interest. To him she would be 'belle of the ball' and, maybe, a judicious conversation with the senior Dancers might gain reward for them all, encouraging them to view him with increasing favour. Hopefully, and happily for him, they would begin to think of losing a high-spirited, wayward daughter and gaining a watchful and careful son. His action would show he was the right kind of young man for Nelly having demonstrated a proper inbred regard for family honour.

Bertram gave a final check to the story, moved a few letters around, and sent the final version to the printer.

The next morning there was confusion in many households when the high society column was scanned for the latest gossip. Over breakfast coffee, readers looked in vain for news of a voyage to accompany the picture of a large cruise ship, but could only find the headline 'NCE Dancers at Sea' followed by a few lines about goings on at a council house. There seemed to be no sense to the article and people quickly moved on to read the next titbit. Bertram apologised to the young photographer for the printing mix up in the word 'séance' and the mysterious disappearance of the photograph. He promised to ensure that it didn't happen again.

As for Nelly, Chloe and Elly – would anyone think they were 'NCE' of the headline? – just in case, they were sent post-haste to join the liner on a short cruise, and, some months later, Bertram achieved his heart's desire and was chosen to be the first son-in-law of Mr. and Mrs. Dancer.

Barbara Griffiths

DANCERS AT SEA

The removal van drew up to the house next door. My brother and I were sitting on the wall between the two gardens as we had done every morning for days awaiting the van's arrival. We had heard that the house had been let again. It was the last weekend of the summer holiday before my brother and I went away to different boarding schools.

"Alike as two peas in a pod," everyone used to say, which annoyed us both. We wanted to be different. In fact, we did everything we could to be different.

I had started thinking of my brother today as I sat watching the auditions for a new musical I was producing. We had, indeed, turned out differently. I was involved with the theatre after gaining entry to RADA and working my way up from sceneshifter, then walk-on parts to actor/producer. I had been flicking through the experience gained by some of the 'hopefuls' auditioning and the fact that one of them had been on a cruse ship started my reminiscing. Tom, my brother, had enrolled in the Navy when he was eighteen although, eventually, he became a Captain of a luxury liner.

The mind is a strange thing – it only requires something small to start off a chain of events that happened in the past. I remember, particularly, the day of the removal van. Whatever differences Tom and I had, we shared one important factor – an ability to see the funny side of life. We had many laughs together, great days of fun – and one of the happy memories was the day of the removal van.

It was fascinating to see the possessions of other people being unloaded and we tried to guess what sort of people would end up being the folks next door. Over the years we had watched many families come and go as the house was only let for six months or a year at a time.

This family was definitely different. There didn't appear to be any children because there were no bikes or prams or things that looked as if we would be lucky enough to have new playmates. Instead we looked on in amazement as we saw a variety of items from all over the world pass by. There was a large fish, something that looked like a shark, in a glass case; a wooden parrot on a stand; African drums; a carved hat stand that looked like an eagle – and tea chests bulging with ornaments; a very big grinning carved mask; large spears and, best of all, a carved figure of a woman – a sort of mermaid from the bow of a ship. We had never seen such an array of curios. Even the removal men seemed amazed. They were grumbling as they carried the mermaid and the taller of the two men muttered, "Strange lot this time, Fred – gives me the creeps!"

We were so excited we jumped off the wall and ran to tell our mother of all that we had seen. Of course, in typical mother fashion, she told us, "Don't be so nosey, boys – and just be sure you don't make yourselves a nuisance. They are probably a perfectly ordinary family. Go on now, out you go to play."

The freedom we had in those days was just taken for granted. We had all sorts of adventures, but this time, after a quick drink and a biscuit each, we returned to the wall dividing the two properties. The removal van had gone and all was quiet. As we looked hopefully at the front door out came the most extraordinary man we had ever seen. He was very suntanned, which was most unusual in April, and wore white bell-bottomed trousers, a string vest, a scarf around his neck and a sailor's hat. His arms were covered in tattoos and, as far as we could see, they were all of a woman's head with long curly hair. He seemed to us a mixture of

Pop-Eye and a pirate. He hoisted himself up onto the wall to sit beside us.

"I'm Jed Hawkins," he said cheerfully. "What are your names?"

Tom whispered to me, "Go on, Owen, ask him if he's a pirate." Then he burst into a fit of giggles.

I managed to keep a serious face and asked the man if he had come from abroad. Then, this very unusual fellow kept us enthralled as he told us of his travels.

Jed was captain of a ship called 'The Castle'. He related tales of dolphins leaping high at the side of the ship, particularly early in the morning. He told us of treacherous storms and how he had rescued people at sea. He even said that he had seen a mermaid.

More giggles from Tom.

Jed told us that he knew of a ship that had vanished without trace. He told of the time he had been attacked by a shark when he was diving for shellfish. The shark had been particularly nasty and Jed had been lucky to escape with his life – he had the scars to prove it. We listened in awe as he told us of all these daring things he had done and laughed at some of the things that had happened. It was already dusk when our mother called us and we reluctantly went home.

"Come and see me again," called Jed.

Promising to visit Mr. Hawkins the next day, we went home. It had been very difficult to get to sleep that night, I remember, thinking over all the wonderful tales he had told us.

Waiting until 10 o'clock the next morning we were only too pleased when Mother gave us a cake to take next door as a welcome gift. We had told our parents that there was a real live sea-faring captain next door – a buccaneer no less – and we were eager for more stories. Tom rang the bell. It seemed ages before a woman's voice said, "It's open – just push."

We pushed. There in front of us was a lady, with long curly hair, sitting in a wheelchair. She had a blanket around her legs and for one absurd moment I thought she might be a mermaid!

"Come in, come in," she said cheerily. "Jed has just popped to the shops for some groceries. By heck, that cake looks good enough to eat."

"How long will Mr. Hawkins be?" Tom put the cake on a table.

She laughed. "I expect you want to hear more of his stories, don't you? – he's always the same, can't resist an audience. But don't believe half of it! Before Jed tells you any more tales I'd better put you in the picture."

She pulled the blanket away from her legs and we saw that her two feet were in bandages. "Sorry to break the spell," she said, "and bring things down to earth – Jed always fantasises. We're retired now and I've had to have my feet done. It's all the dancing, you see. Jed and I have travelled the world as entertainers on the 'Union Castle Line' for fifteen years and my feet really suffered. We were called the Dancing Duo – and that's all we were – dancers at sea!"

DANCE OF THE OYSTERCATCHER

The winter dawn is late. The weak rays of the sun struggle up over the horizon, barely reflecting on the glassy sea and sprawling village. The lights behind some windows dazzle brighter. On this fickle morning the sky is soon darkened by a bruising array of purples, clouding the memory of yesterday's sun. By the time I leave the house the wind has swept in from the east, kicking up restless, frothy waves and scouring the beach of its precious dwindling sand.

The weather suits my mood. I am missing you after your visit.

I have come to watch the oystercatchers. Most days I wake to their family squabbles just yards from the house and always find their feverish antics amusing. They look so resplendent in their shiny morning suits of black and white, stabbing their long red bills at the clammed-shut mussels that cling to rocks for survival. The birds are never still. They dance and hop from rock to rock poking and prying and chattering – then suddenly take off in a whirl of sound, swoop low over the waves and circle back to where they were, to start over again.

I walk along the beach, across peaty weed beds soft underfoot. The draining tide has exposed slimy bladder wrack that oozes its glistening swollen orange sacs everywhere. It slithers and squelches in a way that disgusts me. Why is it here clogging up the middle of the beach? We used to build sandcastles here. Do you remember? And sand-boats – then wait for the tide to launch them. The sides always crumbled, of course, melting in the water like ice cream on a hot day – but that never stopped us.

Caught in the rocks there is a large bottle, not cracked,

not dented, a washed-clean white plastic bottle. I pick the bottle up thinking that wood will warp, metal rust, glass will crack, stone erode, but this white plastic bottle remains almost as perfect as the day it was discarded on some beach somewhere. It is indestructible – in seven languages. On the side is printed, 'No deposit, No return'. No return! Plastic bottles always return. The sea deposits them in thousands – on every coast it visits. There is no message in this one. I check before returning it to the water, watch it dance away with the ruffled tide and think that there must be a plastic beach somewhere in the world.

I had a dream last night. The vivid images are still so real in my head. You were grown, but not yet adult, dancing over the sea, alone but for the sail you clung to. You reminded me of an oystercatcher, the red sail pointing to the wind, and you looking so sleek in your iridescent wet suit of black and white. It seems so silly now as you were definitely moving above the water, not on it, and, to my knowledge, you have never learnt to wind-surf. I remember feeling very calm. Your arms were stretched wide on the sail as it guided you, bobbing and curtsying above the waves, round and round, back and forward, dancing in time to the swaying music of the wind over a vast empty dance floor. I watched you fly further and further away from me.

For a moment, in the dream, I felt so powerful. The longing to call you back was so strong. I thought of altering the past – making you free to dance forever.

But it was a fleeting moment – and I didn't call.

The dream belongs to yesterday – like our footprints washed away after so many tides – like the sand, dredged, to become just a memory.

I watch the oystercatchers for a while longer as they bob and curtsey, as they dart and wheel in the wind from rock to rock and call with a piercing, piping cry to each other.

It is raining now and raindrops are being whipped away from every point of my body, but I am still calm, knowing that calling you could not have changed the past.

Your wings will always reach for the wind to swoop and circle you back to start again.

In my mind, you will always dance.

Pamela El-Hosaini

DANCERS AT SEA

Two small, shadowy figures gathered their burkas tightly around them and with fresh resolve headed into the desert wind. Hidden from view were strained faces, scraggy limbs, torn dresses and worn out sandals. Hunger pains and feelings of faintness slowed their progress, but sheer determination and strength of spirit drove them on.

"You're late today. I feared you would not come," called Abla Zeinab as they huddled into the little room, already overcrowded with eleven other ragged youngsters – eleven other shadows of their inner beings whom the teacher called her little princesses.

"Yes, we had to hide when *they* passed and *they* stopped the truck right by us so we couldn't move until *they*'d gone," trembled Maha. "We waited a long time."

Farida tightened her grip on her sister's hand as she relived the fear of being caught with the deadly contraband of notebook and pencil under her burka. So they froze into the nothingness that was their fate, huddled behind the bombed out village huts, breathing in the sand and insanity around them. A hungry rat had boldly paused to scrutinise the statues of children, and Maha had had to stifle a scream which was whisked away into the desert dust.

In fear and horror, Abla Zeinab quickly moved to the window but, seeing only the shifting sands, she knew that the girls had not been followed and for another day they would not be discovered. Relief mingled with anger and frustration flooded through her, but she said nothing, preferring to hide such emotions from her little charges. She looked at the earnest young faces, individuality alighting on each one as the uniform burkas were briefly cast aside. Knowing there was no spark of hope to cheer the dead days and nights of their young lives, no whispered music in their souls, she was filled with an overpowering urge to rouse them, to set fire to their spirits and force them to demand their rights and claim their heritage.

"My lovely little girls," she thought, *"bereft of dreams and play, placidly accepting – knowing that Islam means 'submission' – but to the will of Allah, not the will of man!"* And all at once Abla Zeinab knew what she needed to do.

"I must break open their prison and set them free, fire their souls, but oh Allah, give me a sign that what I am about to do is right. Show me that what I want is for their joy, and not for myself. Although we are in this sea of misery, we are merely the troubled waves that ride the surface. We have little depth but are united by the still waters of the vast ocean beneath, and what affects one of us, affects us all."

Zeinab's impassive face did not betray to the girls that she was troubled, but a stray sigh escaped her lips, and the observant children knew that all was not right. So ever wanting to please her, they were anxious to begin and with eager restlessness, the girls determined to surpass themselves in their tasks.

"I've learned the *fattah*, reading, reciting and dictation," announced Safia with shy pride. All eyes turned to her with shock. She had never spoken in class before, and Zeinab had almost given up hope that she ever would, assuming that the trauma of witnessing her mother and sisters shot through the head had sent her into an eternally silent world.

"We would be most honoured if you would recite for us," said the teacher gently, trying hard to fight back the tears. In a trembling voice, and with eyelids lowered, Safia faultlessly recited the first verse of the Koran. During the moment of silence that followed, Maha leaned over to her, agog with amazement, and squeezed her hand.

"I didn't know you were so clever," she said. "All the time we were reciting and you wouldn't speak, I thought you were just too stupid, but you're not." Safia smiled, hung her head and blushed with pleasure.

"Il hamdulallah, thank God for this sign," smiled Zeinab. Joy bubbled up within her as she announced defiantly, "I have a wonderful surprise for you this morning. As soon as lessons are done, we will listen to music." Gasps of fear and horror broke out. Ignoring them, she continued in a casual voice, "An old friend from over the border came last night and brought us three tapes."

A hush fell over the class. The girls were partly reassured by Zeinab's apparent disregard for the authority's ban, but each one waited for someone else to take the lead. Eventually Lama blurted out, "That's good, that's veryveryvery good." She was ignorant of what exactly to expect but would have done anything to please her teacher. She also knew that if *they* had forbidden it, then *she* wanted to hear it.

"Il hamdulallah for the rebels amongst them. Not all their spirit has been crushed," thought Abla Zeinab.

There followed a babble of confusion. Excitement mingled with fear rose within each girl, but it soon gave way to squeals of delight.

"I've heard it before but I can't really remember any tunes."

"Well so have I and I CAN remember."

"My big brother used to listen to music all the time when he was my age."

"Well my mother says music is from Allah and they played it on her wedding day!"

"So! My uncle's cousin used to be a MUSICIAN. He used to play the oud and was even on the radio before I was born."

As their enthusiasm kindled, their stories waxed taller and more colourful. In reality, two of the older pupils *had*

27

heard music before but it had been a long time before, and they scarcely remembered.

Farida whispered to Maha in a worried voice, "What shall we do?"

But Maha was already entranced by the thought that she would hear the forbidden sound for the first time. Her mother had told her about it, had even sung a few quiet songs to her when she had been ill with fever, but surely this would be different. The forbidden fruit would taste all the sweeter because it had for so long been denied, talked about only in hushed whispers behind the privacy of locked doors.

"Well, we'd be punished for even *being* here so listening to music won't harm, and anyway, *they* won't find out. Abla Zeinab will look after us."

Farida frowned unconvinced, but seeing Abla's warm and comforting smile, she let her fear float out and disperse into the ever-present desert winds, as she joined in the excitement of anticipation.

"But will Allah be angry with us and send the *Jinn* to throw us into the burning fires?" insisted the last, earnest, wide-eyed urchin.

"Why is he called '*il rahman il rahim*', my dear? It means the merciful and the compassionate. Allah wants us all to be free and full of joy. We are not harming anyone by showing our happiness, and the music makes us joyful and forget our pain. But remember, everyone, this will be our little secret."

Thus comforted by the teacher's words, the last concerns fell silent.

Abla Zeinab scraped the sand from a corner of the room and removed a couple of worn boards from the floor. She lifted out a battered cassette player folded in a faded blue sheet and wrapped in a couple of old plastic bags. Carefully blowing away the sand that had relentlessly drifted into the

28

cracks and crevices, she set the player in front of twenty-six incredulous brown eyes. Silence reigned. The mesmerised girls watched Abla's long, slender fingers slip a cassette into the player and switch it on. Hardly daring to breathe, they strained forward. After some crackling, there was nothing but a whirring noise followed by silence, and a long, thin, brown ribbon began to flow from the player and become more and more tangled. Abla Zeinab snapped it off and started to sort out the confused and strangled mess.

"Well perhaps there was some grit in the player, or maybe the tape was old," she explained flatly.

Eagerness turned to disappointment on every earnest face.

"But look, we still have two more tapes so we'll try again," she said, with far more brightness than she was feeling.

"How can these poor children who have nothing be cheated of even this meagre treat," she thought. *"Bismillah, I must get this thing to work!"*

She deftly inserted the second tape, but this time, after a few stops and starts which produced the usual crackling and wailing, the player began to turn steadily and emitted some high pitched notes.

The silence from the girls in the room was palpable, their tension high. For a full two minutes or more not an eye strayed from the cassette player, not an ear strayed from the sounds. Then the forbidden teacher did a strange thing. She began to clap her hands steadily, in time to the music. At her encouraging nod, Maha, too, began to clap. Lama, Farida, and even shy little Safia followed suit, and soon there was a small circle of girls, wide eyed with astonishment at their own audacity, all clapping their hands in a steady rhythm to the sounds coming from the black box on the floor. Fear had turned into pleasure, and soon smiles and giggles of happy embarrassment filled the room.

But there were still more delights to come! After a few minutes of this, Abla did something that was even stranger and more forbidden. She stood up and started to sway, taking little steps this way and that, moving her whole body in time to the music. Her hand stretched out towards the girls.

"How beautifully she dances," murmured Lama as she reached for her teacher's hand.

Farida gave a start. So *this* was dancing! Eager to try, she too tremblingly rose from her cross-legged position on the floor and began to sway, just as Abla Zeinab and Lama were doing. Maha pulled Safia by the hand and they turned in circles to the tune. Leaden limbs became pliable reeds at the water's edge, billowing seaweed in a fast-flowing tide. Bending and swaying, anemones floating on a summer swell, they danced and clapped. In no time at all, thirteen little bodies gyrated to the wailing sounds. With heaving chests and waving arms they looped and circled in the small room. Surrounding their teacher, they became the planets that orbit the sun, the disciples that encircle the Master. She was the rock; they, ribbons of weed trying to find a crevice in which to safely anchor. Then they lined up behind her and copied what she did in a 'follow the leader' game – a graceful swan, followed by her uncertain little cygnets.

"Did Prophet Mohammed dance too?" wondered Maha, as the tape crackled to an end and they all finally sank in an exhausted heap on the floor.

Abla Zeinab surveyed the scene and knew that she had done the right thing.

"What happy exhaustion! My little dancers at sea," she laughed. "Today we find ourselves awash in this ocean of ignorance and confusion, but one day, order will prevail over the chaos. Goodness and goodwill and compassion will light each one of us, and we will all be called by the voice of Allah, the voice of truth, beauty and love, to witness the liberation of everyone. So we will wait quietly and listen, listen together until we hear the gentle calling, the calling that will free us all from the shackles of poverty, shame, violence and oppression, free us from the vile bigotry that reduces us to nothing. Then you will dance eternally to the wonderful music of life, because somewhere, over a distant and lost horizon, now shrouded in the fog of ignorance and fanaticism, life is beautiful."

"What did Abla mean?" asked Farida as the two small girls gathered their burkas tightly around them and retraced their steps into the desert wind.

"I think she meant we can dance again tomorrow," smiled Maha.

- -

Margaret Rees

NIGHT THOUGHT

The moon is the world's memento mori
slung on a chain of stars.
I am conscious of only my bones, no flesh,
and the skin drawn tight on my skull.

Pamela El-Hosaini

SNAKES AND LADDERS

With pillow damp and head throbbing, Harmony awoke to the high wail of the baby's cry. Tightness in her breasts told her that he'd slept longer than usual but was now ready for his morning feed. Cradling his softness into the crook of her arm, she settled back into the pillows and stroked the downy hair as he sucked and gulped hungrily. The little grunts, as the milk hit his stomach, made her smile. Then she winced with pain as the throb in her head intensified. She tried to piece together the fragments of her interrupted dream to hold them in her slow awakening.

There were flowers, yes sunflowers, that had stretched in every direction, each head swaying with celestial music. Harmony floated above the rippling petal fields, mingling gold with ribbons of coloured notes as she bathed in cascades of music. She dived into the fortissimo breakers and her toes carelessly flirted with pianissimo ripples. Her hair and skin soaked up the melody until she merged with the sounds making one huge vibration that went on and on past all horizons, to the ends of space and time.

Gently caressing the contented baby, now drowsy with sucking, she sighed, thinking that at seven months he should be sleeping longer, allowing her more rest so that these awful headaches would subside. Whispers of the dream coaxed her to remember more, making her relive the terror of the nightmare ending.

In the distance was a coiled, twin-headed snake, streaking crazily towards her, blocking her way. With forked tongues flashing, it defied her to pass, but she'd boldly reached out and stroked the first head until it bowed low. The second, harder to pacify, was soothed with soft, lyrical notes, a humming that came from somewhere deep inside her. As she reached for a ladder to cross the shimmering coils, and catch in her fingers the last notes, a third head, more deadly than the others, suddenly sprouted.

Fangs dripping with venom barred her path and she could hear the music slipping away into the distance, into an infinite future that didn't seem to care that she couldn't catch up, would never be part of. In panic she lunged at the third head with a knife, and as the blood spattered in every direction it let out a wail of anguish. Her trembling hand dropped the knife but there was the stain of its blood, forever on her skin. It was a constant reminder that she'd committed a crime so great she'd spend eternity in a vain attempt to atone. Her stomach churned. Grief overwhelmed her.

"Thank you, little Valdis, for interrupting that one," she whispered to the baby. Swinging her feet over the side of the bed, she suddenly retched uncontrollably, but her stomach was empty. Tears of self-pity stung her eyes as she shuddered at the power of her dream.

Harmony felt better after her morning tea and aspirins and gazed at little Valdis in his highchair, at his laughing blue eyes, his chubby fingers banging a spoon on the tray.

"He has Sergei's eyes," she thought. "Oh Sergei, look at our wonderful little boy, the treasure you never knew we created together. If you can know now what I'm thinking, let us sense your presence; let us feel your love and comfort and protection. I'll do my best for him, for both of them. I'll do it for them and for you. How I miss you, miss our life together, miss you more than ever."

It was the same melancholy thought she had every morning, some days with greater intensity than others. Sometimes she railed at Sergei; railed at God for that dreadful day fourteen months – or was it fourteen years – before, when he'd stepped under a bus and out of his body. His eager, precious life had been snuffed out, just like that, and his black cello case was spattered in sticky, red-black

33

blood. It still had the stains on it when they returned it to her, still had the crusted dried blood on it now, up in the attic. She just couldn't bear to wash it off. It would have seemed like washing the last traces of *him* away. But what was the use of going over and over it in her mind . . .

"C'mon Mummy, we'll be late again. 'Member the one in the blue chair gets to be princess."

Harmony smiled at Katya who was pulling on her Oxfam anorak, pulling at her mother's hand, then pulling at the pushchair holding Valdis with the kicking legs.

"Look, he's a footballer. C'monnn Mum, we want to go. First there gets the blue chair."

"Yes, Princess, we'll make sure you sit in the blue chair today."

They stepped out into the chill autumn morning, into the damp mood of Forest Hill. Grey terraces spread out in every direction, and Harmony was glad that the mothers' and toddlers' playgroup was only a few streets' walk away.

Katya jumped and skipped over the cracks in the pavement.

"Princesses can't step on the cracks, Mum."

"Really, will a big wolf come and eat them up?"

"Nooo, silly. The cracks are the bad snakes. You slide down them and have to go back 'til you find a ladder to go up again."

Harmony gave a shiver as she once again remembered her dream: bliss swallowed by a nightmare. She wondered what it all meant.

At the hall Katya skipped off happily in the direction of the bouncy castle, the blue chair quite forgotten. Harmony pushed Valdis towards the kitchen and joined her friend seated intimately close to the tea and coffee urn.

"Thanks, Pauline, just coffee though. I really must stop the biscuits or I'll never get any kind of waistline back. So much for breastfeeding!"

Pauline smiled. "Don't worry, it takes a while. He's only

34

seven months and you were *really* big carrying this time. It took me a year to even start to feel human again, and now Jasmine's two and I'm back in a size ten."

Sipping her herbal tea, Pauline continued, "The problem's your aura, darling. You're just not centred yet. Not that I blame you, of course: too much in a short space of time. Did you try those aromatherapy candles I told you about?"

Harmony sighed. "Well actually I find Wax Lyrical a bit on the dear side . . ."

"Of course, darling. Don't we all! But there's that cut-price stall in the market that sells those bottles of essential oils. They last for ages. A mixture of lavender, geranium and ylang-ylang does wonders for me . . . but maybe you should leave out the ylang-ylang, you know, just for now."

Harmony flushed. She hadn't told Pauline about Olav, her one lifeline. He'd been Sergei's friend and played second violin in the orchestra. They'd arrived together from Latvia, with the same yearnings, the same ambitions. Harmony thought back to the day she'd met them. It had been Olav's boisterous laugh that she'd noticed first, and only later surrendered to Sergei's quiet sensitivities and passion. United in grief over Sergei's sudden death, once a month, for the last four months, Olav had taken her to a concert. Days of preparation and planning preceded each date. A flurry of charity shopping to find that 'extra special' something to fit, wash and alter, plans for a baby sitter from the 'mums in touch' group, and special treats for Katya so that Harmony could clear her conscience enough to leave her for the evening. Afternoons were spent walking Valdis in the park to 'tire him out' and ensure that he slept while she was at that magical interlude in her otherwise dreary routine.

Olav inspired her, nourished her dreams, believed in her. He would say, "Harmony, it wasn't for nothing that you

35

have this name. Believe me; I've seen many at the Yehudi Menuhin School who weren't a bit as good as you. Keep practising and even if you play with a small orchestra, or do part time, you can't give up your music. Neglect such talent and it will die. It will evaporate with your soul. Please promise me that you will practise every day."

Strangely, when she was with him, she exuded confidence and knew that she was capable of anything. Olav was her path of escape, and she believed that with his help, she would somehow get back on track, make up for the lost musical years and rejoin her burning passion. With him she could unfold her postponed ambitions as easily as she took out her carefully laid away violin, and give vent to the hopes and dreams inside her. She smiled as she remembered the last month's concert. On returning, Olav had insisted that they play Beethoven's Violin Romance together. Enraptured by the music, they were both transported to a capricious place where whimsical was fashion and immediate was essential. It was only natural that when the violins were laid down, they too would lie together. It had seemed right that, while the children slept, they ended up in one another's arms, each seeking comfort from the loneliness of their lives. It was a shared dream, almost a shared destiny.

"So why the faraway look in your eyes, and what are you smiling and blushing about? I don't believe you've heard a word I've said," coaxed Pauline, trying to untangle the fringe on her scarf from the ankh pendant around her neck. "Share the secret."

"Oh it's nothing, Pauline, just a dream I had last night." Harmony mechanically pushed at the pushchair to encourage the sleeping Valdis as she looked down at her mud-spattered sneakers. "Disturbed me, really. Wonderful music, then there was this snake, and I held a knife and there was blood everywhere. I woke up feeling all hot and bothered with a killer of a headache. Then I threw up."

"Hmmm, very Freudian, I'd say. Now, you are keeping your 'dream journal', aren't you? That Jungian analyst I told you about will want to know all the details. By the way, you know what today is, don't you?"

Harmony looked blankly at her.

"It's your 'M' day. The Message! Remember the spiritualist meeting I took you to last week? The medium there, the one I had such good vibes from, said that by today you'd have a clear indication of what your future path should be. You know she told me about the 'new force' that would blend into *my* consciousness, well I went for an Indian head massage and there he was . . ."

"Oh, a new man?"

"I simply couldn't believe it; he was just too sublime . . ."

At this point Pauline's voice took on a distant quality, like an actor playing a part on a faraway stage. The occasional words such as "authentic, enlightened, and *terribly savant,* darling" entered Harmony's awareness, and she was able to give the occasional grunt to keep the conversation going. Her mind, however, was occupied by the usual tug-of-war dilemma. Should she put Katya into pre-school, find a child-minder for Valdis, and return to her music? She surely wouldn't be any worse off financially than now, with just her social security payments to live on. At each monthly concert with Olav she knew that her music was her life, but when she looked at the children she wondered how she would ever be able to go on concert tours; leave them for endless hours without her, and she without them. Yet the longer she dallied, the harder it would be to ever go back. Silly Pauline had convinced her that for a mere five pounds a medium would facilitate a message from Sergei, and enlist his help with the decision. But it had all been too vague and disappointing, and she had left the séance with the feeling that his presence hadn't even been there.

"Well, what do you think I should do?" demanded Pauline.

"Oh I'm terribly sorry but you lost me there for a moment," stumbled Harmony.

To her relief, a small hand tugged at her jeans and she realised that the playgroup was over.

"Mummy, can Patsy come over and play today?"

"No, not today Princess, Mummy's not feeling too well. She can come next week. Did you get to sit in the blue chair?"

With a wide-eyed blink, Katya ran back into the hall and jumped into the now vacant seat, announcing to one and all that she was Princess Katya, and with a wave of her magic wand would turn all the snakes into ladders.

On the way home, Katya chattered happily. "No snakes, Mummy. Walk on the empty bits! To market to market to buy a fat pig, home again home again jiggedy jig," she sang as they turned into their street.

The postman had left the usual array of unsolicited loan offers, a book club brochure, a red electricity bill and a postcard from a friend on holiday in France. No message there. After preparing a lunch of baked beans on toast for them all, Harmony turned to her horoscope in the free Dulwich weekly.

'Pisces – *What you want possesses you but don't risk losing the treasures that you already have. These are cathartic and creative times. Are you the reason for all this movement or just a passenger caught up in it?'*

"Well that certainly fits. And I do have two wonderful little treasures . . . Many would give the world to have what I have . . . Time flies, and maybe a couple of years won't matter too much. By the time Valdis is in school I'll get back to serious study and have more time to practise."

Harmony felt happier. Even the sun managed to peep out from behind a cloud, so she opened the French windows from the bedroom into the tiny rear garden and led the children outside into the sunshine. Her head started to ache again so she sank into the faded deckchair and was soon drifting away, oblivious to the squeals of play.

"Mummy, Mummy it's the doorbell. Come and answer. Someone's at the door."

Pauline stood on the step with little Jasmine awkwardly straddling one hip. Her free hand held a Boots' bag containing a small box.

"I've been a bit worried about you lately, Harmony, so we were just on our way to the shops and I thought we'd call in for a chat."

Over coffee the two friends unburdened themselves. Pauline talked animatedly. In contrast, tired and jaded Harmony constantly played with a wisp of her auburn hair, twisting it around her finger. She found it an effort to follow the conversation until Pauline presented her with the box. She gave a start as she read the label.

"But it's impossible, I'm breast feeding . . . and my periods haven't even started again yet!" she faltered.

"Yes but that doesn't matter. It's not a hundred percent you know! And the sickness, I had it too. Look, just take the test and then you'll at least know if you need to *do* something about it."

Fumbling fingers unwrapped the box, took out the strip. Minutes later they stared in disbelief at the unmistakable double pink lines. Nothing could have prepared Harmony for this moment. She swayed. So Olav, her saviour, was now her destroyer. His tales of belief in her, his frustration at her unused talent, his wooing, had all propelled her along the path of ruination. A cold wave of hatred raced through her veins. She hated herself for being weak. She hated Sergei for abandoning her. She hated Olav for his seduction. She hated Pauline for making her aware of her condition. She hated Valdis for not allowing her to sleep, and Katya for being born and forcing her to give up her dreams. Harmony's wild expression confused and frightened Pauline.

"You say it's a man called Olav? Well, I mean, is there any chance that he would . . . you know, if he were to . . ."

"Take me on? With three children? Ha! He's married, Pauline, married to his dreams. He's the one who preaches that there's no room in life for children and a career. He's dedicated to his violin, in love with his music. He's going on a world tour with the orchestra next month. No room for anything else. *I won't even tell him!*"

"Look, Harmony, it's not for me to say, but there's this new kind of termination available; just a pill at night and the next day you have not much more than a heavy period. Just like the 'morning after' pill really. I'll come with you. Let's get the kids' coats and we'll go to the afternoon surgery, speak to your GP." They stepped outside in a confused daze, Harmony's mind reeling.

"Careful, Mummy, you're stepping on them. Don't step on the cracks or the snakes will get you."

The three-headed snake! Harmony looked down at Katya, all rosy cheeks and pigtails, stooping down to adjust a Velcro strap. One hair bobble was threatening to fall out and the green anorak, the too-big, unzipped, shabby anorak, was falling off one shoulder. Harmony stopped. She thought of snakes and ladders, music and children. And all at once she knew – the third snake!

Her two beloved babies were a gift, the melody of her dream, loved more than her music. Would she be up to the challenge of the third, the one that truly barred her way? A silent tear escaped. She could cry now, but not all her tears. Save the rest for catharsis and creation. Stopping to hug Katya to her chest as if she would never let go, she was overcome with love and burst into joyful laughter. In a flash, the pain of her indecision was gone.

"Thank you, my little messenger. Mummy will be careful

not to step on the snakes. Let's stop at the shop and get you some Smarties, then we'll all go home."

"Mrs. Polly had a dolly who was sick, sick, sick," sang Katya.

"So she called for the doctor to come quick, quick, quick," joined in Harmony, as they all danced home.

- -

Margaret Rees

A HOUSEBOAT REVISITED

The "Glasgow" is held fast in the river mud
Which, softly silting, inches up her sides.

            Do you remember
September mornings when gold dripped from above
And swirled up from under? We ate on deck,
The sweet milk sharp with cold on our teeth.
The ducks came begging for breakfast and you, dear,
Fed them with half a loaf – and we with no bread –
And kindly made sure the slow, old, weak, lame
Or otherwise unsatisfactory got their share.

Strange that our love should also have foundered.

David Griffiths

TOO MANY OATS SPOIL THE BROTH

Someone had suggested the dregs of porridge.

Whilst the idea had come in a roundabout way (because the conversation had been about wallpaper – or it could have been broken china) he felt it was like a divine voice to his soul.

He drained off the juice from what was left of the solids, having eaten the rest for breakfast – and dinner – and tea – because he had misread the directions and mixed far too much.

The dog had not been much help, turning up its nose and its stomach contents after the third bowlful; it may have been too much salt or too little sugar, or the animal was getting over-fussy. However, he felt that one positive learning aspect was that he now knew the dachshund's capacity was about 1.5 bowls of porridge. The dog had been an object lesson to any postal service with its swift and careful placement of the excess requirement. Unfortunately, the soggy white pile had been deposited on a part of the carpet that had previously been unmarked, but he believed that, in time, it might match the interesting pattern of various shapes and hues caused by other untimely accidents.

The dachshund's hair was of a similar colour to his own, or what was left of his own. Just before Christmas, as he had faced the usual early morning shock of looking at himself in the mirror, he had realised with horror that he was thinning on top. He saw that his weight (mainly round the middle) was increasing and his once luxurious mane was rapidly decreasing. Whatever the cause (it could have been the strain of the village hall renovation) he knew he had to act before all was lost.

The shaggy coat of his pet had not been easy to shave – but the two bald patches would soon re-grow. He had not intended to nick the dog's skin as he looked for the right shade and length of hair, and had been taken by surprise when the animal had shown a previously unknown side to its character. The stitches in his hand could be removed in a few days, so he was told, and he hoped the scar would not be visible for long.

The porridge juice felt quite sticky. It would surely do the job. He spread the glutinous solution to his bald patch then carefully applied the dog hair. With some difficulty he placed some of it in little bunches, but they either stood up too straight, or gave up the struggle rather easily and lay down like dead thatch.

Combing it caused a slight problem. The teeth of the comb soon clogged and also made winter-like furrows on his pate. But he wasn't over concerned about these for, although they went over his head in a slightly different direction, they nearly matched his forehead frown marks.

Porridge solution set, and satisfied with his handiwork, he set off for his nightly walk with the dog. All went well – until, unfortunately, a sudden shower caught him with nowhere to shelter.

The distinct creamy dribble down his face caused by the blend of rain, milk and porridge, along with a familiar taste of salt and sugar, told him that his repair work had failed.

Walking home, he realised it couldn't have been divine inspiration after all. He may be a terrible cook – but, more likely, God knew porridge wasn't hair glue!

Margaret Rees

WAITING FOR FIREWORKS

Lottie looks at her friend anxiously, with a mixture of admiration and the familiar sense of guilt. She and Cara have known each other for more than sixty years since they met as debutantes when that word still had magic for girls of well-to-do families. They were chaperoned at cocktail parties, danced at the Trocadero, spent long weekends in country houses and took motor trips to Biarritz. Today, they sit in Cara's private drawing room, two ladies of comfortable means, sipping the champagne the hotel has provided as a millennium gift for its residents.

Cara is still striking in her regal way, and for all her more than eighty years she keeps a straight back and a decisive way of speaking. Her sleek hair is as purely white as it was once densely black, her brows and cheekbones as clearly defined as ever. She is newly coiffured, elegantly dressed in evening purple, and expensively perfumed. Lottie recollects how Cara chose that scent to be her own and how all her life she has been able to ensure a lavish supply. First her admirers, then her husband, now her nephew – men have always spent freely to please her. Just at this moment, Lottie observes, Cara is making no secret of feeling rather bored. Perfectly still and impassive, she gazes out at the dark promenade and the small lights bobbing in the wind, waiting for the fireworks to begin.

Lottie is also elegantly dressed, but less distinctively than her friend. She wears an embroidered silk blouse in eau-de-nil with a toning wool skirt. A cashmere cardigan hangs over her shoulders and pearls gleam inside her open collar. Her permed curls are soft grey, rinsed with a touch of blue. Eighteen months younger than Cara, Lottie has always played the role of little sister, which suits her temperament as much as it reflects the difference in their ages. Hardly more than a schoolgirl when they first met, she was flattered by Cara's apparent interest in her, and fascinated by her sophisticated manners.

It is clear and always has been, especially to Lottie, that in this friendship Cara has the upper hand. What Cara wants, she obtains; what she suggests is agreed to. As usual, Lottie watches her, ready to do little tasks, trying to please, trying not to irritate. She chats about the other residents in the hotel, and about the staff and their shortcomings. She pours the wine, placing a napkin so that Cara's silk velvet jacket will not be damaged by an accidental splash.

When the telephone rings, Lottie readily gets up to answer it. It is for Cara, of course; why should it not be? This is, after all, Cara's room.

"It's for you, dear. Peter."

Cara seems pleased to hear from her nephew, now middle-aged, but still her favourite. Her brother died many years ago and her sister-in-law always bored her, but Peter, who teases and flatters her and who hopes for an inheritance, is always welcome.

She stretches her hand to take the telephone from Lottie. "Peter, how lovely to hear you! Are you coming to relieve our tedium? I wish you would, darling . . . Lottie and I are just yawning at the sea with no-one for company but all the other old trouts . . ." She enjoys using the teasing words that she knows he will appreciate and is rewarded by his laugh and reassurances.

As Cara chats, Lottie's thoughts turn to another New Year's Eve, 1939. She sees in her mind's eye the two young women in the Mayfair service flat which belongs to Cara's father, but which is, to all intents and purposes, Cara's own to live in as she chooses. The modern décor and furnishings,

45

the gramophone, the drinks tray, all testify to her stylish taste – and to the wealth needed to indulge it.

Cara is at her dressing table, struggling with her jewellery. "Help me – I can't fasten this dratted necklace!"

Lottie helps, pressing the clip of the amber beads together and deftly fastening the fiddly little catch of the gold safety chain. She is bubbling over with laughter and excitement. It thrills her to be going out with her dashing friend, into London's fashionable night-life, among wealthy young people caught up in the early months of the war but not yet accustomed to it, not knowing that the end will not be soon.

Colin, Cara's adoring lieutenant, briefly on leave from the army, and Lottie's own admirer, Paul, are coming to take them out through the darkened streets to dine and dance at a smart night club. Behind the blackout curtains, and to the accompaniment of the latest music, they will greet the first New Year of the 1940s.

Lottie's beau, Paul, an American ten years older than her, is in England to complete a business deal with her father. He is kind and good-looking and she has really become very fond of him; she knows that he dotes on her – his "little English rose". He is also rich and generous, buying her anything that she wants, or that he wants for her. He has already asked her to marry him and go back to California with him, but she is not sure – not while London is so exciting!

As usual, Cara looks elegant in tailored black satin, her dark hair sharply cut. She gazes at herself in the mirror, then turns her neck, glancing sideways to check the effect of the amber earrings.

Standing behind Cara, Lottie sees her own image, softly pretty in pink chiffon and pearls. Cara's reflection speaks to hers.

"Darling – how nice you look! Are those the birthday pearls Paul gave you? He really must be gone on you!"

"Well, yes, he does seem to be – but I'm not sure I should let him buy me such expensive things. After all, we're not engaged – at least, not yet."

"Why shouldn't he give you nice presents? It obviously pleases him to spoil you and with all his cash I envy you your luck. Enjoy it!"

"Oh, Cara, you don't need to envy anything of mine – you are so clever and good looking, and . . . I don't know . . . you talk to all sorts of people and make them laugh . . . you dress marvellously and you've got this place all to yourself."

Cara gives her a saucy look "Yes, well, that does have some advantages when one wants to entertain, let's say, a friend!"

Catching on belatedly, Lottie blushes. "Cara – you know I didn't mean that!"

Still lost in the past, Lottie shakes her head in amusement, recalling her twenty-year-old self. Strange, she thinks, how things turned out. Her eyes on the dark window where the fireworks will soon blaze, she remembers that long ago New Year.

New Year's Day was just dawning when Colin kissed her. Paul and Cara were dancing at the far end of the room – Cara had swept him off, declaring that he had lavished quite enough attention on Lottie, and now it was *her* turn.

When Colin told her he loved her, Lottie could not believe it at first. He had seemed so devoted to Cara, whether she noticed him or not. Lottie felt as though she had stolen a precious possession from her friend, but when, a few delirious days later, Colin asked her to marry him before he went to North Africa with his regiment, Lottie did not hesitate in saying, "Yes."

Lottie was surprised and pleased when, in early summer, Cara married Paul and went to live with him in the ease and safety of California.

Before 1940 was over, Lottie, a bride and a widow within the year, found slight consolation in the commanding officer's kind letter, which told her that, before he died, Colin had known that he was the father of twin girls.

Even in the first agony of her bereavement the twins were Lottie's life, a joy to her that had never faded, even now they were middle-aged ladies with grown families of their own. To keep her babies safe and at her side, Lottie had left war-time London and lived in the old Suffolk house with her parents. She learnt to grow vegetables and 'make do', focusing her dreams on her two darling girls. During the war, and in the grim years of rationing that followed, Cara's parcels and the brief, scribbled cards that came with them gave glimpses of a more colourful world than grey old England in the late 1940s.

"My dear," Cara wrote, "we hear that you can't get nice things to eat on your coupons, so I hope you enjoy these. Paul and I are celebrating Christmas with his parents in Baltimore – comfortable, of course, but very boring. We'll be glad to get back to San Francisco. Sometimes I envy you the blitz! My love to your parents and the girls . . ."

Lottie gave the cards to her little girls to stick in their scrapbook, so that she could still see the idealised pictures of American family bliss, but no longer read the words.

Then, wealthily widowed in 1955, Cara returned to London and started a successful business importing American cosmetics for the London stores. Lottie, living again in the London house with her two teenage daughters, was always at her friend's service. She was always ready to help Cara in any crisis, or with any boring task. At Cara's behest, she would make up the numbers for dinner or bridge; she would address invitations and Christmas cards;

she would stay in for repair men; she would even answer the telephone to discarded lovers, quickly learning to let them down as gently as possible.

For her part, Cara was an enchanting and generous friend to the twins, who sometimes wished that their mother had half Aunt Cara's glamour. Lottie was aware of this and slightly resented it, but, bound by the old fascination, she could never refuse Cara or even challenge her. Besides, Lottie admitted to herself, Cara's vivid life gave her own rather humdrum days an interest and a purpose they would otherwise have lacked.

Rousing from her reverie, Lottie hears that Cara is finishing her telephone call. "So, darling, we'll see you here soon? I'm counting on it . . . take care. Happy New Millennium to you, too."

Cara passes the telephone back to Lottie and picks up her glass to taste her champagne. "Ugh! Flat and warm. Pour me another, won't you, if you haven't guzzled it all."

Lottie pours for Cara and sips from her own glass. She picks up the conversation again, as usual deferring to Cara's interests.

"So, Peter is coming to visit. He really is an ideal nephew – almost like a son. I've always thought it was rather selfish of Paul not to want children."

"My dear Lottie, whatever gave you that idea? Paul wanted us to start a family as soon as possible – but I couldn't bear the idea. Babies – ugh – so messy and demanding! So I told him I couldn't – and I took good care not to."

Lottie stares at Cara and finds it impossible to respond to this revelation. She has always thought that her own happiness had been secured at her friend's expense, but over the years, she considers, she has done much to repay the debt.

Now, to Cara, she says, "If only Colin had not been killed, I would have loved to have more babies."

"Dear Colin, how handsome he was . . ." muses Cara. "You remember that New Year's Eve when we went out with him and Paul?" She continues nonchalantly, as if amused by the memory, "That was when I told him I didn't love him, and never could – I saw him making up to you just to get back at me, to show me he didn't care, the silly boy! And then marrying you to stay close to me! But I escaped to America with Paul – in fact, I planned that things would turn out the way they did – and it just suited both of us, really, didn't it? I managed it so well – me with dear old Paul and his dollars, you with your darling babies. And the funny thing is we each think we got the better bargain! Dear old Lottie, all these years you've done everything you could for me – I suppose to atone for stealing Colin from me. But you didn't steal him – I gave him to you."

Lottie's eyes widen, her face loses its colour, and, for a moment, she appears about to choke. Then, abruptly putting down her champagne glass, she begins to shake and gasp with short, tight bursts of laughter. She catches Cara's astonished gaze, now turned fully upon her, and holds it.

"You gave him!" she shrieks. "How could you? After all this time, how can you brazenly tell me that you were then, and still are, a devious, scheming, heartless bitch? After all these years, when I have done nothing but love my children – Colin's children – and be a friend to you – even if what you say is true, why tell me now?"

As she sobs, Lottie sees the first salvos of the firework display, muted by the double-glazing, shoot into the sky behind Cara. She takes a deep, shuddering breath and uses the wisp of lawn and lace that she always carries in her sleeve to wipe away her tears. She can see quite clearly through the window that the whole of the sky above the promenade is lit with multi-coloured stars, cascades of fire and spinning wheels throwing off great glowing sparks which die in an instant. Her anger flares up like the sparks and dies as quickly. She has made an astounding discovery. She stares steadily at Cara as she speaks.

"You've set me free!" she exclaims, "and I'm going to take this gift – just as I took the other one – and make the most of it in whatever time I have. Good-bye, Cara. Enjoy your New Year!"

As Lottie steps into a taxi soon after midnight on New Year's Day 2000, she looks up at the hotel window one last time, and sees Cara sitting alone, staring out into the empty night sky, waiting.

But the fireworks are over.

TALENT

I laugh,
I cry,
I talk a lot.

I walk,
I sing,
I eat a lot.

I don't write,
I don't paint,
Nor sew a fine seam.

But I'm not lazy,
I don't sit and dream.

I work in my kitchen,
I do love to bake.

Hope my epitaph will be
'She could make a good cake.'

Linda Dobbs

THE INHERITANCE SHELTER

Billy Clifford bequeathed his worldly goods to his only child on his seventieth birthday. He believed that having survived his allotted 'three score years and ten' it would be comforting to ensure some good would be passed on to the offspring and his grandchildren whilst they were young enough to reap the benefits. Billy Clifford departed this life, due to entirely natural causes, at the stately age of ninety-three and three quarters, little realizing that the intervening twenty years would swallow up what he thought was some considerable wealth.

After the solemnity, pomp and joy of a memorial service committal, supported by the regional Salvationists, Audrey Gibbs sat down with her family to read a simple will, which confirmed that all her father's investments, savings, and personal effects were hers to dispose of as she saw fit. The contents of Billy's sheltered accommodation flatlet consisted of a bed, a gas cooker, and a battered rocking chair, which Audrey fondly remembered had comfortably held the two of them sixty years ago whilst Billy read to her from Golden Bible Stories for Children. She had boxed up several books, odd china and cutlery, faded family photographs, and ancient holiday souvenirs. Billy's presentable clothes had been bagged up for the next Salvation Army jumble sale. An old biscuit tin, wedged into the back of the dusty airing cupboard, contained four and a half thousand pounds in used notes.

Audrey found several pictures of her mother, Eleanor Clifford, taken in the early days, long before she had lost her mind and been institutionalised. And there were her mother's and Billy's Salvation Army medallions, prayer bookmarks, Sunday school record cards and a tea chest crammed with editions of 'War Cry' published between 1946 and 1951. William Clifford had been a staunch Army recruit way back in the early thirties and had remained loyal to the cause through to his dignified end. Audrey was quite taken aback to find that Billy's will had specified the Army should care for him in death, even as it had, so surely, cared for him and Audrey after Eleanor Clifford's mental breakdown. Though what level of care Audrey had received was dubious, she now reflected. Audrey recalled very clearly the household moves there had been to all areas of Britain, when her mother was well, which took her away from chapel choirs and the singing she loved, uprooting them every eighteen months so that Billy could continue his ministry within the Salvation Army. Never had they managed to settle, and it was only with the hospitalisation of Audrey's mother that Billy finally conceded it was time to call a halt to the campaign and entrench himself in the activities of an Army hostel in the centre of Swansea. Audrey had married into a Gower family and been close at hand to see to it that her father ended his days with all comfort and care imaginable, through the local authority.

Now she was determined to put what little of her father's wealth remained towards an appropriate reminder of him. She had in mind a little house, built with her father's legacy; a house which she could call her own, which she would never have to leave, unlike those earlier homes before and during the War, which were never so welcoming as the one she had made for her three daughters and husband Ken above the bay at Horton.

She found the ideal octagonal summerhouse in a November issue of 'The Garden' and fell in love with it, immediately setting out a long list of specifications to ensure it fitted into their immaculately groomed rear garden plot: cedar larch lap with five of its walls half glazed and the three back walls solid to provide shelter from the prevailing wind which blew over Port Eynon Point from the west, and up the Bristol Channel. Window catches and door furniture were to be in brass, to give an illusion of warmth. The sisal matting and sun lounger chairs heavily upholstered in chintz buttercup regency stripe percale would bring sunshine into the house on a dull day. Ken was informed that he'd have to install lighting to the little house and that Billy Clifford's cuckoo clock (a souvenir from his Lausanne honeymoon) would need to hang on the back wall so they wouldn't ever forget how Audrey had come by her garden retreat.

Watching the erection of the summerhouse, Audrey was unexpectedly saddened. It was rather like a replay of Billy's funeral. Like a sexton, the contractor came to prepare the ground, and dig the footings. Precise measurements, tidy removal and redeployment of topsoil, and some ready mixed concrete materialised into the summerhouse foundations.

The following week, all the component parts of the little house arrived and the erectors huffed and puffed their way from the lane up into the back garden with each wall section, the window frames and the eight roof sections, countless nuts and bolts, and the brass fittings which gleamed in the early spring sunlight. Audrey reflected that the pallbearers had found it hard to lift Billy's coffin. He might have been ninety three years old but had lost little of his six feet-two and fifteen stones stature; a mighty man, always in full command until the end.

The compact summerhouse was bedded in and firmly anchored, its pre-formed glazing panels were installed, and the roof was finally battened down after about two days. Audrey had insisted on a weather vane to grace the apex and the chosen Shire horse silhouette rotated gently in the late spring breeze blowing across the Bay, as she gazed admiringly at the finished building.

After much rearranging of the sun loungers, some considerable regret about her decision to include the noisy cuckoo clock, and then guilt at having such an undaughterly thought, she brewed a mug of tea in the kitchen. Wearing comfortable carpet slippers, she strolled up the garden, tea in hand, to sit in the little wooden and glass box, firmly dismissing the image of Billy serene, white silk framing his face, in the Killay undertaker's Chapel of Rest.

She reflected on the activity of the last few days and looked out over the close-cut lawn which ran right up to the door of the summerhouse. She held the mug to her lips and whispered "Thank you, Daddy. I couldn't have done this without you."

After living a daughter's early life under so many roofs, she had finally come to rest in her father's house. No-one would ever make her forsake the inheritance shelter.

Linda Dobbs

BLACK MOUNTAIN SQUALL
(Dedicated to Miriam)

It was a first for me, too!

I wanted to show you
the obstacles we could hurdle.

How could I know your blood
would almost curdle,
when the gale buffeted us so?

I would never have let you go.

Then we reached a meagre haven,
heard the croak of a lofty raven.

We sheltered huddled on cold stone,
our experience of life grown, yet again,
on that mountain bright and wild.

– Your relief palpable, you smiled!

Mike Roberts

THE MILKY WAY BENEATH MY SEA

Youth's magic memories are profound
With Horton Beach my playing ground
And here my great discovery
A million stars beneath the sea!

Dragnetting on an August night
Half-tide, ebb's good, we'll be alright.
The sea is warm, the fish are free,
A million stars light up the sea!

Phosphorescent waves – blue-green and white –
Along the bay make ribboned light.
The deep-end two release the net
To merge with stars we can't forget.

Fifty yards of curving net
With bobbing corks and poles erect
We drag a hundred yards or more
Then check the starry catch on shore.

Four times we drag the ebbing tide,
Pick up the bags, there's more inside
With sole, plaice, sea-trout, bass and ray
From the starlit world beneath the bay.

Tho' well past three, awake I lay
As golden moonlight swathed the bay.
Oh, dragnet fishing's part of me
In the Milky Way beneath my sea.

When my life's journey here is done –
Some battles lost some trophies won –
Then I'll ask my God to bury me
In that starlit world beneath the sea.

Frank Thomas

MARTHA'S LUCK

Martha had never married. Indeed, she had never considered the idea that she might even have a relationship with anyone. As a child she must have at least witnessed other children playing together, laughing, enjoying moments in time. But if she had, either she was incapable of having such feelings or she had been force-fed by her parents over the years into the mould that now encased her. Her parents had died long ago, but she lived on, seemingly unqualified to experience any variation on the hum-drum.

In a small Victorian terrace house in Stockport Martha lived as she had always lived. So far, the house and its neighbours had escaped the slum clearance schemes that were changing so much of the town. The war had long ended and England was trying hard to change its old ways, its conventions and its expectations. The furniture in her 'two up two down' had not been changed nor had any other of her apparatus of living except for items that had worn out. Even when artefacts had reached the end of their days she would replace them with identical items. It would not occur to Martha to replace a worn-out saucepan with a pressure cooker or to supplement a dustpan and brush with a vacuum cleaner (or a 'Hoover' as Martha would call it). She seemed almost unaware of the technological revolution that had gripped our western world's imagination in the decades following the turmoil of World War Two.

She ate, she slept and she cleaned. Oh, how she cleaned! Every morning she washed, she put clothes on and every night she took them off again. Martha had no-one for company and took no apparent interest in any changes going on around her. She had no hobbies to pass the time, no crusades to fight, no family to visit and no friends – only acquaintances.

Strangely enough, however, Martha never seemed to suffer from depression or boredom or even envy of other people. Her life just moved quietly, day by day, month after month, year by year, from birth to an inevitable death.

Then one day, Martha's unvarying predictable routine varied. It was as if the world had stopped turning unexpectedly and with a clash of gears had resumed turning in a different direction and at a faster speed. It must have been the disruption caused by the fact that school holidays had briefly changed Martha's daily timetable of activity.

She had visited her local supermarket at her usual time, when normally it was quiet, to pick up her weekly supply of fresh but traditional foods – nothing trendy or sophisticated, of course. Quite unexpectedly, an atypical and unconscious impulse, while queuing to pay, made her look at and read the notice beside her. The queue was long and to fill in the time waiting, for possibly the first time in her life, Martha broke with habit and acted on that impulse.

When she reached home she stored away her purchases, folded the plastic carrier bag and carefully filed it away for possible use at some future date. Putting her purse in its proper place she remembered her uncharacteristic lapse in the shop and felt, momentarily, rather ashamed and a little perturbed.

The following day was Sunday, the only day of the week when, having more time on her hands, Martha always bought and read a Sunday paper – albeit with great detachment. Sitting down in the kitchen next to the old black-lead range with the newspaper beside her and the washing-up after her meat and two veg completed, she put on her spectacles – unreliably repaired with cotton – and started to read. Occasionally, her eyes closed and then reopened after a short spell of half sleep. Then, having read the weather report and other useless data, her eyes lit on an item she had never noticed before. She looked at it for a while with little or no emotion. Finally, she reached out for her purse, took out a slip of paper and then re-read the news item. Never geared to quick reaction, decision or even excitement, Martha accepted the fact before her and lay back in the chair to consider the novel situation. She turned over the slip of paper in her hand and, after peering closely at the small print on the back, absorbed the information.

It appeared that with the marked numbers on her slip of paper and a telephone call, she would be a millionaire several times over.

Martha sat there pale and transfixed for hour after hour, thinking as she had never thought before. It must have been eight o'clock that evening when she stiffly rose from her chair, dropped the slip of paper that threatened her life into the fire and contentedly put the kettle on for a nice cup of tea – the same brand of tea that she had drunk for fifty years.

Tarrick El-Hosaini

FOR PALESTINE

In my fist I clutch this stone,
And bravely stand my ground alone.
Whilst tanks and troops roll forward still,
Their march to crush my hand-held will;
"But why obstruct our right to peace?"
I ask the brigade of armed police.
Their answers in the guns they wield.
Palestine's holy ground
"Will she ever be whole and healed?"
Her history, drenched in blood and tears,
Calls out to the mass of heedful ears;
Much-deafened by her silent plight –
A pill too bitter – too ugly a sight!
So join with me in quiet prayer
For justice and for peace: free and fair
For a Palestine without divide,
For a Palestine we all can share . . .

Linda Dobbs

THE FITNESS EXPONENT – ABSOLUTELY TYPICAL?

Miss Charlotte Sims-Green is a pro-fitness queen,
who works out in nylon and leather.
Her exquisite figure exudes health and vigour.
As she moves, she's as light as a feather.
Five feet two in slouch socks, her red bootee Reeboks
are threaded with star-spangled laces,
and her thonged unitard sometimes struggles quite hard
to keep dynamic breasts in their places.
Below belt, *derriere,* Charlie takes utmost care
to restrain ripened 'glutes' in tight Lycra.
So she works on bum squeezes whenever she pleases
 – mostly driving to work in her Micra.
With tattoos on triceps and bronzed, bulging biceps
and a headset mike tuned to loudspeaker,
she puts folks through their paces, causing many red faces,
proving she's top dog – they're all much weaker.
In between frowns and pouting, as she cues you in shouting
a routine for high impact kickers,
she will scrunch her bleached hair, elbows high in the air,
and then modestly adjust her knickers.
She pulls bands. She hefts weights.
She has mauve in-line skates
and a routine for adductor lunges
which blokes think is painful, but they're never disdainful
when she's sporting a neckline that plunges.

Miss Charlotte Sims-Green wouldn't ever be seen
in a gown, for she hates to be formal.
She prefers fleece to viscose, wears a tracksuit to discos
and feels 'birthday suit style' is just normal.
She wears Dunlop and Nike, owns a red Triumph bike
which she rides at events in all weathers,
where she swaps workout gear, puts a stud in her ear,
and flashes cute all-in-one leathers.
Charlie's skin is like silk. She drinks pints of fresh milk,
every day, to keep wrinkles from forming.
And she's up with the lark, jogging twice round the Park,
half-asleep, trying to stop herself yawning.
For it's tough at the top and you can't ever stop
and your image demands snappy fashion.
Take a tip from sweet Charlotte,
who's a 'moonlighting' harlot,
and make Lycra your number one passion!

Mike Roberts

EGGED ON

In my Horton boyhood memories June is the month of sunshine, new potatoes, flowers and swimming.

I woke to the sound of kitchen noises – my mother lighting the fire and getting breakfast. I cleaned my teeth and washed quickly. "Don't forget to wash behind your ears!" I wondered why – no-one ever looked behind my ears. It was Sunday morning, time for clean shirt and socks, new sandals bought for Easter, always Clarks with a pattern of holes in the top. Sunday morning was Sunday School in Horton Chapel, although on days like this the beach, the valley, the cliffs and our numerous secret dens were more attractive.

We always arrived early; the Chapel was never locked in those days. Once or twice we found the organ unlocked too, and pedalled away with the organ going full blast – only to be caught red-handed by the organist, an elderly lady called Miss Glance, who shouted at us angrily with the look of an indignant buzzard that could have killed a rabbit on sight. Talons weren't necessary. Like frightened rabbits we sat in silence while she told the Minister and his daughter, our Sunday School teacher. We were duly reprimanded.

Sunday School consisted of drawing, the story of the day, and hymns. After the story of the day, we would try to catch out the Sunday School teacher – "Who did Adam's children marry?" "Who cleaned out the Ark?" "Why did Jesus turn water into wine – the Minister said wine was wrong?" The teacher would patiently explain that alcohol was bad for your health – "If you drop a worm in alcohol it will die!" "When our dog had worms, my dad got tablets from the vet," Jim said. The puzzled Sunday School teacher announced the next hymn.

We had a secret in the Chapel. There were loose screws at the back of the organ and we could squeeze a hand inside and push the stops out. When the organ was opened and the organist saw that the stops were out she would exclaim that someone had a spare key to the organ and had been playing it without permission. She would rush off and complain to the Minister, while we ran outside, hooting with laughter. So the phantom organist of Horton was born, while we watched the proceedings with delight and wide-eyed innocence.

After Sunday School, it was home for lunch quickly consumed and off to the beach. Our swimming trunks wrapped in towels, we rushed to the beach, changed in the dunes and dashed into the crystal clear sea which always seemed clearer and bluer than ever before. "Let's see who can pick up the most pebbles" said Jim, and the four of us dived and dived until we were exhausted. "Let's see who can stay under longest." This usually ended in an argument over the length of a second – some people's counting was faster than others. Then, four skinny, shivering boys smelling of sea and dripping with water would plunge into the warm sand. We ran our hands through it, hoping we would find money like the old men who roamed the beaches in high winds – but we never found any! Then we would look for new adventures – jumping off Big Top (the highest dune), seeing who could jump the furthest and how long we could stay in the air. There were always arguments on these points. Exhausted, we slowly dressed.

Just as we were leaving we saw three of the girls from the village walk into the sand dunes. We ducked. "Let's hide their clothes," said Ken. We thought that was a good idea. As the girls ran down to the sea, we crawled through the dunes to find that they had brought two of the farm dogs with them. We knew all the dogs in the village – they were our friends. They came to greet us, wagging their tails

– they must have wondered why we were on all fours like them! As they returned to the shade of the nearest beach hut, Ron had a stroke of genius – "Let's dress the dogs in the girls' clothes!" We all laughed at the prospect. Coaxing the dogs, we attired each of them in bra, pants and blouse. Then we waited for the girls to come out of the sea and sent the dogs down to meet them. The girls shouted in horror as they reclaimed their clothes from the mystified dogs, while we jumped up and down, yelling in delight from the safety of the dunes. The girls threatened us with death – they were much older than us and could hit hard, so we kept a safe distance.

We decided to go back to our roadside den near the bus stop and ambush German tanks in the desert. Someone said, "There aren't any trees in the desert," so we settled for Normandy. "Let's play parrots." Parrots was a well-established game we played in the sycamore tree. As people, usually old ladies and gentlemen, walked to the bus stop, we would perch high in the tree and imitate the loudest macaws. The victims would look around trying to identify the source of the noise while we giggled with delight. We would call the old ladies by their Christian names – strictly forbidden! "Hello smelly Nelly!" She'd look round angrily. "Does she ever smile?" asked Ken, "I wonder if we tickled her under her chin like a baby and went 'coochee-coo' would she smile?" Someone else said, "We could tickle her moustache!"

Today – Sunday – there were no buses, and no targets for parrots. We climbed down to resume the war against German tanks – the day trippers' cars chugging wearily up the hill. As we crawled into the bushes, Jim exclaimed, "Look! A chicken has been laying in the hedge – nine brown eggs." Someone suggested, "Sell them to the trippers." "No, they may be addled – anyway they're not ours." But then one little genius said, "Let's bomb the

German tanks!" The plan was agreed – a totally new war game! We passed the eggs up the tree into a hollow which was an old barn owl's nest. One of us, now in the RAF, crawled along the branch above the road and waited. An old angular car struggled up the hill, moving more quickly as it approached Fern Bank. The egg fell behind the car – splat on the road! We waited for another car – the egg landed on its roof! We were delighted but worried in case it stopped. However, it droned away to Horton Cross and far-off Swansea. Another car – another mess! Soon a large old square car, fawn with big mudguards and tinted windows, came along. The 'bomb' was released and – disaster! – fell right on the windscreen. We were terrified as the car drew to a halt by Morgan's Farm and an elderly man and woman emerged to examine the damage. As they walked back down the road, we climbed higher up the tree, completely hidden in the broad sycamore leaves. They peered upwards, "Nobody here," they said. At that moment Jim, whose inspirations were totally unpredictable, started clucking like a contented hen. His hen noises were supreme. The man and woman roared with laughter. The man said, "Well, well, well! I would never have believed this if I hadn't seen it with my own eyes!" We clapped our hands over our mouths until the car drove away, then howled with laughter as the driver and his wife returned to Swansea to entertain their friends with the tale of the amazing Horton hen.

After this close shave, it was down the tree and home for tea. "What have you been doing?" "Nothing" was always the reply but the wrong answer. Mother never missed a thing. "You've got green on your shirt and your hands and knees are dirty!" My hands and knees were always dirty. Sometimes I licked my hands but my knees always gave me away.

On Sunday evening we would go down the hill to see my aunt and my Grandpa at "Sunny Bank". I would sit in silence and listen to the tales of long ago from the family and friends who always seemed to be visiting. Grandpa, in his eighties, seemed older than time and always complaining that things were going from bad to worse. Electric lights? "They heat people's brains – it's not natural." Flushing toilets? "Unhealthy!" His earth closet remained in the garden until he died. "Why is the government giving away the Empire? Mahatma Ghandi can't run a country – he can't even dress himself properly!" Grandpa talked about everything, but things were always worse than they had been in the old days. "Too many foreigners!" – he meant anyone from Swansea or beyond.

Then, after our Sunday visit, we would walk up the hill, my legs aching. I would clean my teeth and go to bed, another summer Sunday in Horton at an end. From my bedroom window I would look over the sea, the sparkling stars and the distant lights of Ifracombe, the owl hooting in the background. I slipped into a happy sleep, a Horton dreamland of sand, sea, sun, and seaweed. The world of my boyhood seemed endless.

Reni Stableforth

LOW TIDE AT HORTON

The rocks are a grey solid tide
Where no sun
Lights the sandgrains
Beached between.
Tawny weeds
Stitch boulder to boulder,
Smooth pebbles stir the selvage
Of the receding sea.

A solitary gull skims rocky clefts
With arrogant cry
Above some bright flotsam
Begging reclamation –
Such wanton
And alien presence
Becomes beach-comb treasure
Until the tide's turn

Vernon Griffiths

THE TOTEM POLE

Things were not going well at all. Already Silas John was beginning to sweat and he had barely been on stage for a moment or two. Silas knew how vital it was that he and his audience got on well together from the word 'go'. Everybody agreed it was so important to a comic's self esteem. But whatever confidence he had, it was about to be shattered into tiny pieces all over the orchestra pit. No orchestra pit, though, in this club, just a little space between tables to house a beat-up piano.

Silas didn't wait for a laugh when the punch line came and went. He raced through his routine as if hell-bent on self-destruction. When the curtain closed, he raced back to the dressing room that once had been a toilet of distinction. At least he had something to sit on.

He pulled at his case which was firmly wedged between the pedestal and the pipes. It looked like a case worthy of Masonic association. But, for Silas, it was more important than that.

He opened the lid gently and gazed in awe at the miniature totem pole lying protected by blue silk. Just one foot long, but it looked impressive all the same. Silas took hold of it as if it was the most precious thing in his life. He couldn't stop looking at it.

He placed it on what he considered to be a position of importance – in the middle of the toilet seat cover. Then, back to the case. Beneath the silk lining he felt for the replica tomahawk – actually it was no more than a toy hatchet he had acquired after a visit to a local hardware shop. It had the air of being a magical shop from a bygone age.

Even though space was restricted Silas performed a reasonable war dance in front of the totem pole. He waved the hatchet as menacingly as its size allowed; it snapped in half, but the adrenalin started flowing again for Silas. Gone were the miseries of his stage performance – somehow or other, as if by magic, Silas was restored to his former confident self.

But then Silas pulled himself up sharply. What the hell was he doing? Was he reliving a childhood dream about 'Cowboys and Indians'? If anybody glanced in the toilet, what would they think? It could easily end up with yet another comic being safely locked away in some remote home.

Silas John went over the times when he had stepped on stage at the club. Lousy jokes for a lousy audience – jeering, slow handclap – all had led to an urge to do something out of the ordinary. The totem pole, complete with silk-lined case, had originally been bought for his teenage son who also loved cowboy films. But its beauty had stirred something deep within Silas. The toy hatchet was a mystery. He had gone into the shop just to buy a tin of paint and come out with the hatchet – but no paint. Now he must get a replacement.

Silas looked at his watch. He had an hour or so to go until his next performance. He slammed the toilet door behind him and raced out into the street towards the shopping centre. The hardware shop was nowhere to be found. He searched and searched until he remembered that next door to it he had noticed a hairdressing salon with the strangest of notices in the window – 'Come in and enjoy a hair-raising experience'.

Silas was a reasonably quick thinker and put two and two together. A hair-raising experience – a toy hatchet – a totem pole! And then he gulped. It could only mean one thing – what, according to the movies, Red Indians did best – scalping! What was it all about? He had to find out.

Eventually he found the hairdressing salon with the strange notice still in the window. But no hardware shop next door – only an Indian Take-Away! Silas took all this in his stride. It could only be for the best, he thought. He didn't really need the hatchet any more.

By the time he returned to the club he was bubbling over with enthusiasm, and his second performance that night turned out to be a great success. The world was, from then on, a better place for Silas John.

S.J., as he came to be known, now regularly appears on television in his own show. The opening credits have a distinctive feature. They appear over a wide-screen shot of his completely bald head.

Dead centre of his pate is a very unusual tattoo – a Totem Pole.

Margaret Rees

SONNET

*"I know a lady in Venice would have walked barefoot to
Palestine for a touch of his nether lip." Othello Act IV sc.iii*

Venetian girl with smoothly plaited hair
And a proud profile like a sharpened knife,
The casual record of your long despair
Summons the burning moment of your life.
Perhaps you envied Desdemona's fate,
Who loosed love's falcon at a nobler prey,
And put to scorn the customs of the state,
And died for love. You would have gone her way
But though you would have welcomed every shame,
Each stone, each rut, each insult on the road,
And chosen so your passion to proclaim,
You were too slight to bear that tragic load
For tragedy's the birthright of the great
Not to be purchased at a lesser rate.

Barbara Griffiths

TOTEM POLE

It stood there tall and imposing,
So straight and proud like a tree.
The face was dark and fierce
And seemed to be looking at me.

I thought of Cowboys and Indians,
Old films that I used to see.
War dances, shouting, fighting –
Was that face looking at me?

The fine wood was carved in detail,
Telling tales of mystery.
Shivers ran through my body;
I felt sure t'was looking at me.

I knew it had special meaning
For those who truly believe.
Shadows leaping and dancing,
I feared it was looking at me.

Its fate was – sale in an auction
For all to make bids and see.
A sad end for such splendour!
I knew it was looking at me.

The bidding then slowly started –
It topped two hundred then three.
I heard "Sold to that lady."
It was coming straight home with me.

I duly paid up the money,
Amazed this happened to be.
I looked again at this treasure
And I was sure it winked at me.

Tarrick El-Hosaini

MISCONCEPTION

For justice and for freedom: the true American way,
We wage this war with terror, for a peaceful future day.
Our tanks and bombs, we all are told,
    "Must root out that evil foe."
    "We'll rout him from his hole,"
    and proudly this to show . . .
    "That all might see that villainous wretch
    We before our billowing flag did fetch!"

Imagine this:
    The wealthy earth in stripes of white and red,
    More bright than snow, more crimson than we bled.
    By fifty stars the night shines bright,
    All reverence to our patriotic might!

    What need then, of our mountains, fields and seas . . .
    When, had she air, the moon too could feel her breeze.
    For each is but a star, reduced in self same manner,
    By stately weave into our brave celestial banner!

But thinking on:
    This miraculous world about, our planet rich and rare,
    Holds such abundant mystery
       that all mankind might share . . .
    In praising God, and building up a heaven of His earth,
    Where all are members, free by their sacred birth.

The war is won:
   With bombs and terror our minds were primed,
   Weapons were hidden that none could find . . .
   And now our justice met, and toppled is that Man,
   Brought down is the villain, with his evil plan!

But who backed Our Man until he'd served their scheme,
Which once fulfilled's abandoned now,
      and changed is that regime?
So maybe from the Pentagon, a message to every land:
"Your President utterly lost should be,
      but for his helping hand."

And do you find, hidden behind
      your stately White House walls,
That on stone deaf ears their sorry plight falls,
While ever sanguine global voices,
      against that dumb decree,
Cry out with passion for this earth, for you, for me?

David Griffiths

AUTUMN LEAVES

Autumn had fallen with an aching, heavy dullness. The streets, stores, hovels and houses groaned under the drab, doleful, deadness of the season. The city reeled under the onslaught of the dying leaves, the swiftly baring branches, the hard driving rain and quickly darkening nights. This pre-winter period had not crept in like a timid and trembling deer, but swooped like an eagle firmly clutching its prey in the grip of deadly talons.

The sombrely dressed people, hurrying to and from work, tried to remember the sparkling fullness and dress of summer, now torn apart with wild, shrieking gusts that spitefully attacked all in their way. There had not been such climatic drama for many years and the city did its best to shine in hope of better times to come. But it could not cheer the heart or soul of those looking back with longing to the lazy, hazy days of summer.

The lights of shops and streets shone fitfully through the gloom of damp and fog. They offered little comfort, for they were but as transient fireflies. Coloured traffic lights blinked as if in pain, knowing that worse was yet to come. Tall grey buildings vainly stretched upward for hope and help, but only found themselves crushed by low-hanging clouds.

The city wept. Its grief racked the cracked pavements and the dark tear-stained roads and silently sobbing walls sank into sleep and sorrowed in dreams. It was as if its life had ceased, for no longer did it pulse with the throb, vigour and energy of one newly come of age. It was a warning sign as bleak as seen in any prison camp.

It was a place to avoid – for now.

But after rest from the tearing, wearing excitement of busy, people-filled days, the city would rise again from what seemed to be a sleep of death.

It would dance with life, like bobbing, flowered heads of spring – sing its gentle song of welcome to all who come to visit.

- -

Margaret Rees

ORDERS

My master has given me orders
To go on a perilous journey,
Not the safe lowlands and fat pastures
Where until now my meadowed life has lain,
But to climb reluctant over the valley's end
Where teeth of granite menace
The softened flesh and mind,
Where eyes, following the eagle's swoop,
Draw the faint limbs to fall.
True, the views are fine,
But the lungs labour and the heart pumps hard.
And then, my journey's to no known end.
No little town, sun warmed and mountain sheltered,
Is my destination; my orders are
To journey to the limit of my strength,
Test mind and heart against the hardest climb,
Test to destruction. That done
Only to see in space-black skies
How far more bright the sun.

AMEN CORNER

Amos pushed the heavy oak door closed, shutting out the damp February wind. The smoky atmosphere in the room was worse than usual making him cough as he approached the bar.

"Smoky in here today, Jed."

Jed was already pulling Amos' pint. "It's the east wind, Amos, blowing down the chimney."

"Seems worse than usual," grumbled Amos. "Wood's wet I'd say."

The preliminaries done Amos jammed his pipe between his teeth.

"Bert's late," said Jed, placing Amos' pint in front of him. "Or are you early today, Amos?"

Amos grunted, paid for his beer and crossed the empty bar room to the corner by the fireplace. He wasn't early, he thought, Bert was definitely late. Anyway, it wasn't a crime to be early was it?

He settled into the brown mock-leather chair that Bert claimed as his own every Sunday and supped his first pint of the day.

"Back in a minute, Amos," shouted Jed as he moved through to the lounge bar.

"I'm not deaf," Amos shouted after him.

Sunday lunch was being served in the lounge. Amos could hear the hum of conversation, the clatter of cutlery on plates, the clink of glasses and, now and again, a loud guffaw of laughter. He wasn't hungry. He'd been suffering with indigestion since getting up this morning and hadn't been able to eat his breakfast. The meaty aroma wafting through to the bar was doing nothing to whet his appetite. In fact, he didn't feel that grand at all and probably should have stayed at home, but he'd thought a pint or two would help to settle his stomach.

The chimney was still belching out smoke-signals, irritating his cough, but Amos was determined not to move from the chair in the corner. He had as much right to sit there as Bert, he thought. Bert was much too fond of claiming things by right of being the first-born.

The skin of Amos' face prickled with beads of sweat. He didn't really feel hot but he slipped his coat off anyway, deciding to leave his hat on, just in case his head caught a draught from the chimney. Breathless and wheezing loudly he kept his teeth firmly clenched on his pipe as he slumped back in the chair.

"'Bout time you gave up that old pipe," said Jed as he came back into the bar. "I could hear you coughing from the lounge."

"Disturbing the peace was I?" Amos rubbed his chest. "Perhaps you should tell them in there to keep their noise down so that an old man can enjoy his Sunday pint without being forced to listen to their chatter and clatter."

Jed laughed. "Which side of the bed did you get out of this morning?"

Amos didn't reply. He lifted his glass and carried on drinking.

Halfway through his pint, the bar door swung open letting in a blast of cold air. It was Clem Watkins, still in his farm overalls and muddy boots.

Now that's odd, Amos thought.

Like Amos and Bert, Clem always changed into his 'Sunday Best' after morning milking was done. All three of them went to early Evensong together, claiming that a few hearty 'Amens' was a good way to start the week.

Even odder, Clem took off his old cloth cap. Clem never took off his cap – it was generally joked that he went to bed in it. Even odder still, he didn't head for the bar where his beer was being pulled. Clem was not a big talker, but he never, ever, uttered a word until he had downed his first pint. Today, he went straight towards Amos in the corner and sat down next to him.

In surprise, Amos removed his pipe. "What's wrong with you, boy? Are your feet stuck inside those muddy boots?"

Clem took a deep breath. "Got a call from Mary. She needed help to get the cows in from the top field. Just been round to your house. Thought I'd find you here when you didn't answer. You're early today, Amos."

Amos stared at Clem. He had never heard him string so many words together. He wondered why Mary had rung Clem, and, why hadn't Bert fetched his own cows in, and, wasn't it a bit late to be fetching them in for milking anyway? Amos didn't wonder why his sister-in-law had not phoned him, as they hadn't spoken for years over some long forgotten spat. Over the years, she had tried to split Bert and Amos up without success. Both brothers were insistent on their Sundays together. Amos rubbed his chest again. This indigestion seemed to be getting worse. He growled at Clem.

"Why is everyone so concerned about me being early? Do I have to ask permission, now, to leave my house? Anyways, I am not early. You are late. And Bert is very late." He jammed his pipe back between his teeth.

Clem hung his head and appeared to be trying to strangle his cap. He cleared his throat. "Yes," he said, but didn't elaborate.

Amos nodded his head towards the bar. "Beer's going flat over there."

"Right," said Clem. He went to collect his drink.

Amos heard the clink of coins dropping onto the bar as Clem, as usual, hunted for change. Clem and Jed were talking but, strangely, their voices sounded very far away. Amos's head was feeling fuzzy. He rubbed his forehead as if to clear the fuzziness. Perhaps he'd had too much beer on an empty stomach, he thought. And, far from settling the discomfort, it seemed to be getting worse. Taking a breath was difficult. He couldn't get enough air. Suddenly, he felt very sick. He stood up quickly . . .

Clem and Jed were talking quietly, their heads close together over the bar.

"Mary asked me to tell him, Jed, but I don't know how I'm going to do it."

Jed thought for a moment. Then, "It's going to be a shocker however you tell him, them being twins. Perhaps it would be best to just come straight out with it."

The thud and sound of breaking glass seemed all the louder for their whispering. Clem spun round.

Amos was sprawled face down over the low table. His beer glass was in pieces around him. His hat, which was still on his head, was soaking up the spilled beer.

It didn't take Clem and Jed long to realise that Amos had gone the way of his brother. There was nothing anyone could do for him now. They placed him tidily on the floor and sat close to him, too shocked to speak for a while.

Jed spoke first. "Well, you won't have to tell him now, Clem," he said quietly. "I expect he's found out for himself."

Clem, still clutching his cap, said nothing.

Jed spoke again. "Maybe this was how it should be. After all, they arrived in this world together and, maybe, it's fitting that they leave together."

Clem glanced at the empty corner seat.

"Amen to that," he said.

Barbara Griffiths

WHAT'S IN THE BOX?

It was the first time that we had been together for nearly fifteen years. On that occasion my wedding had brought us together – a wonderfully happy day, as most weddings are. I had been able to face my cousins with a smile on my face.

"Lovely to see you – thank you for coming." I greeted them with the usual pleasantries said at the traditional welcome reception line-up.

I had never told my husband of the arguments and fights within my family. Telling someone else made it all sound so petty – and it was. Fortunately, we all lived so far apart that he never questioned our lack of contact. Looking back, now, I realised how foolish my relations had all been, and all over bricks and mortar.

As a child I had loved the stories my mother told me of the magical time she and her two sisters had in their family home. They had had complete freedom to run and play in a field attached to the large house in Wiltshire. The house had been called 'Chantreys'. I had felt as if I knew every nook and cranny of the house, and the garden that had boasted a tree house with swing underneath. It had sounded like every child's dream.

During my mother's childhood my grandparents had rented a cottage in a small French fishing village called Penerf in Brittany and for five years the family had spent very happy times there. My grandmother was quite a character and had been known for cycling around the village waving a fresh baguette shouting 'Bonjour' to everyone. Her French had been erratic, usually stilted and slow, but after a few glasses of wine she became fluent – adopting the correct facial expressions and arm waving to make her seem like a local. She had had a knack of making everything fun for her young girls and they loved it.

Eventually, the three sisters went to university and had then moved on to different careers. The family holidays stopped but my grandparents loved France so much that they had decided to sell the Wiltshire house and buy the cottage in Penerf. The cottage, then, was very primitive and needed much work, but this was to be their project and they had made the decision to make France their home. This was quite an unusual thing to do in those days and the three sisters, Anne, Jane and Beth, had not been at all pleased. The girls had wanted to retain the 'Chantreys'. It was so special to them and they had been unable to agree with their parents about the permanent move. Unfortunately, a huge family row had developed with the result that Anne and Jane determined never to visit their parents. As for my mother, Beth, she had fully realised that she was going to miss them terribly, but she had had to accept that it was their life and their decision. She had tried her best to persuade the other two to see this point of view, but the resentments had grown out of all proportion and all sorts of accusations had been made. It became a really bitter family feud.

The move to France took place and my grandparents had settled and been extremely happy. Even when my grandfather died my grandmother had stayed and continued to enjoy life. Sadly, my mother was the only daughter to visit, occasionally, the home in Penerf. The bitterness grew over the years and Anne and Jane never visited or forgave their parents for selling the family home in Britain.

Throughout this time, the three sisters kept only limited contact, managing to attend each other's weddings and send cards and parcels when their respective daughters were born. So, although I had two cousins, we had not had much contact. Not once had there even been a Christmas get-together and it was just pure chance that we three cousins had ended up at Bristol University at about the same time. But, I feel ashamed to admit, we had just not got on; somehow the bitterness of our respective mothers had rubbed off on us and, although we had seen each other on campus and social occasions, we had tended to avoid each other as much as possible. We simply had made no effort to become friends and after university we'd lost contact completely.

Now, we three cousins were meeting again. We had been summoned to a solicitor's office under circumstances that, as yet, had not been explained. Our grandmother had died a few months ago at the age of 87 and, as the three of us sat waiting, we all unburdened ourselves of our sense of loss. We each felt regret that we had not known or enjoyed our maternal grandparents more. Of the three of us, I was the only one who had been to Penerf and seen their enchanting home. We pieced together the missing years and realised, with sadness, that our mothers had lost almost a generation of family love and unity – over silly, selfish arguments.

Eventually, the solicitor entered the room and offered us a greeting as he sat down. Very deliberately he placed a plain wooden box on the table in front of him. He explained that this was a slightly unusual bequest pertaining to our grandmother's last will. Our grandmother wished him to read out her instructions – which were written as follows.

'Dear Mr. Wilson – as you will know, I have nothing that my daughters would wish to have and there are no personal possessions that I wish to leave to them. As per my instructions, I wish this wooden box to be opened only if my three granddaughters are present together – otherwise my instructions are void. If the three girls are present then the contents of the box may be given to them unconditionally. Thank you for attending to this matter.'

The solicitor looked at the three of us and said, "The instructions are signed by Mary Edwards and witnessed."

For a moment, we all stared at the box on the table.

"What's in the box?" I asked.

Mr. Wilson had taken a key from another sealed envelope. "I don't know. Shall we open it and see?"

With great ceremony he opened the box and placed it in front of us. Inside was another envelope. I opened it. It was a letter from our grandmother.

I read it aloud.

'To my dear granddaughters – I cannot change the past, but, with this, my bequest, I hope with all my heart and my love for you that you three young women will change the future. Your grandfather and I worked hard to renovate our original little home here in France and the other two cottages that are now linked with it. I would like to think that all three of you will take your families to Penerf and make up for the lost time of the past years. With my love – your grandmother.'

My two cousins put their hands into the box and brought out three keys.

Each one was labelled 'The Chantreys' and numbered – 1, 2 and 3.

Pamela El-Hosaini

FORMER LIVES

Lizzie tore all but two of the double pages in half, and rolling them up carefully and exactly, she lined them on the hearth like a row of soldiers. When the entire newspaper had been thus rearranged, she folded the ends of each rolled up page towards one another and tied a knot firmly in the middle, tucking the ends neatly inside. The remaining two pages were then crumpled up with great vigour and laid in the grate. Over this were placed the wadded pages, and finally she criss-crossed two layers of stick on top. Lizzie felt satisfied that she wasn't using too many sticks. Although ignorant of the origins of paper, she could never feel right about people cutting down trees to watch the sticks burn in a grate. It was something she didn't quite understand about the tree's spirit, and whether or not it went to heaven. After all, she'd once reasoned to herself, trees have lives too. So she carefully struck a match and watched the edges of the paper curl up, enjoying the sudden burst of heat that reached out to her. The coals were deftly plucked from the scuttle one by one, and arranged first carefully, then thrown on, as the heat became more intense and the sticks began to spit and crackle. Unhooking the little, black, hand brush, she swept the splinters and coal dust from the hearth into the polished brass shovel and threw them onto the expanding fire. Returning everything to its own place, she gave a satisfied nod.

"Started first time today. It always does when you fold the papers right." With thoughts turning to the immediate needs of the kitchen, she glanced at the grandfather clock in the corner. It was five to six, and time to put the porridge on.

Upstairs in his room, Rob Hetherington reached down

and ran his hand along his leg. He looked out across Port Eynon Point and shuddered at the thought of the blinding flash that had engulfed him, the searing pain, the total blackness. Still, he was alive. He was the lucky, or perhaps unlucky one. He would certainly live, for now, if this could be called living. With one leg amputated below the knee and the other so badly scarred and burned he doubted if the pain would ever go away, he wondered bitterly why his life had been spared, and for what purpose. Falling back onto his pillow, blue skies overtook him, acres of plains studded with lazy sheep rolled out before him, distant white-capped mountains blurred the horizon, and he was on his horse again with both feet firmly in the stirrups. The annoying flies swarmed around the bobbing corks on his hat, trying to find a way in to suck out the salt from his sweaty brow. With a jerk on the reins he led his horse towards the coil of the river. There was just enough time to catch a fish before making camp for the night.

The gentle knock on the door of room 2 of the Hollies failed to awaken him at first. But slowly his consciousness left the blazing warmth of the outback and awakened to the grey, drizzling, winter dawn of Horton. In recoil, he remembered his present situation.

Lizzie waited a moment before opening the door with the breakfast tray balanced precariously on one arm.

"There now, Mr Hetherington, I've brought you some nice hot porridge and toast. You are going to eat a little bit today, aren't you? Got to get your strength up, you know."

Rob glanced at the shy, dark eyed girl at the foot of his bed. "Just put it down there, Shelagh. I'll eat it later."

"No, Mr Hetherington, Matron says I've got to make sure you eat a little bit today, even if I have to feed it to you myself. And I'm Lizzie, not Sheila," she added shyly.

Rob smiled despite himself. "All girls are Shelagh where I come from."

However, the explanation was lost on Lizzie, who only thought how strange and confusing that must be.

During the days and weeks that followed, Rob began to look forward to Lizzie's visits, and teasing her brightened up his day enormously. For her part, Lizzie was drawn to this big blonde foreigner in a way she found hard to understand. Living just half way up the hill with her mam and Aunty Bethan, she found constant excuses to be at the Hollies. Even on her day off she could be seen in the garden or on the sand dunes in front of the Red Cross house, and never had her mam found her so willing to go and draw water from the well at the bottom of the hill.

Winter became spring, and first snowdrops then crocuses and daffodils pushed their spiky leaves through the warmer soil and into the light all over the village. Lizzie had begun to bring some of her treasures to Rob, and each had its own story to tell. First it was just a piece of driftwood, worn smooth by the sea. Unwrapping it carefully from her hankie, she stroked it and explained that it was part of a treasure chest, long sunk on a pirate ship that was wrecked around at Culver Hole.

"Look at these rusty bits, Rob!"

She felt herself flush at the thought of being so familiar as to use his Christian name even though he'd been telling her for weeks he would no longer answer to Mr. Hetherington.

"You can even see the place where the nails were holding the chest together at the corners. This chest was full of coins that came from Spain. But the gold came all the way from America. And you know the name of the Captain? It was Captain Blythe – the cruellest and wickedest man of his time. All his crew were scared of him, especially Joe, the galley boy. He used to shiver whenever he saw him."

Lizzie's eyes grew wide as she stared into space and went on with her story.

"He used to throw sailors overboard just to teach the others a lesson and make them obey him . . .

And when we were little we always minded our mothers because they used to threaten us with Culver Hole. *You do as you are told* they used to say, *or we'll leave you over in Culver Hole and the wreckers will get you.* That used to frighten all the children round here."

Oyster shells that were really mermaid's mirrors, seagull feathers, bits of worn out fishing nets and brightly coloured pebbles all had their stories to tell. As the windowsill of room 2 became more and more cluttered with the flotsam and jetsam of the beach, so Rob's spirit began to mend. Little by little, Lizzie's presence was saving him from the despair he had felt. Dreams of the outback became less vivid and heartrending, and the present situation of being in Horton took over more and more of his thoughts. He was now able to walk with crutches, and he spent more and more of Lizzie's days off sitting on the sand dunes and listening to her tales. The war seemed a very long way off.

"Mam, do you know anything about Australia?" Lizzie had innocently asked one Sunday as she watched her mother's reflection adjust its hatpin to go to chapel. The brow wrinkled into a frown. Annie Evans hadn't liked to be reminded about skeletons in the cupboard, and being an honest Christian woman from the Eynon family, who didn't like to break any of the Ten Commandments, she evaded the question. But Lizzie had noticed the moment of unease, and by the end of the day had wheedled the secret from her mother. So, her great Uncle Bob had been sent out there on a ship as a young lad for stealing a sheep!!!

But he had been wrongfully accused, concluded Annie's earnest and sentimental reasoning, while Aunty Bethan had excused him saying that his poor mam was giving birth to his seventh brother and the other six were hungry with nobody to provide for them after his dad's accident and untimely death.

Lizzie took all this to heart in a very serious way. But perhaps her mam's great Uncle Bob hadn't ended up in hell after all, because Lizzie knew deep inside that God would understand how hard it must have been for them all – what with the new baby and all. And she was sure that Australia must be a very nice place from what Rob had told her.

"I might have cousins in Australia," she told Rob one warm day in May. "Yes, I do have cousins there."

Sitting on the harbour wall by the Salt House, resting after a long and painful walk along the burrows, Rob's aching armpits told him he'd come further today. He was making definite progress. His eyes misted over as he gazed towards the horizon. A million miles from home, yet he seemed to feel very much at home whenever Lizzie was around. Her tanned face, deep set eyes, the gentle curve of her lips, the way she held the back of her hand to her mouth whenever she giggled, all seemed so natural and familiar to him. Even her unruly black curls, which had a life of their own and refused to stay under a headscarf, were just the way they should be. He couldn't quite reconcile how he would leave her, yet he knew that this could neither continue, nor develop into anything lasting.

Lizzie chatted on, failing to notice that anything other than physical pain or aching limbs was troubling Rob.

"My mam's great Uncle Bob was sent to Australia for stealing a sheep. He went on one of them big sailing boats full of prisoners, and some of the men had been murderers too. But my mam says they accused him wrongly and I don't think he really did it. No, the Eynon family wasn't like that even if some of them were hard up and in trouble

94

and all that. Aunty Bethan thinks it was on account of all his little brothers and the new baby and his mam being on her own . . . I think he was innocent though. Must be awful to be accused of something you haven't even done . . ."

Her voice trailed off as she noticed his strange expression. His blue eyes turned dark and his rugged features twisted into a different, yet more familiar face. Glazed eyes stared out towards a distant horizon as his voice took on a more familiar, sing-song rhythm.

"You don't understand. It was hell. Seeing Mam struggling with all us kids, straight from birthing little Billy, trying to help with the oysters, and dad buried the month before. I'd lost my job fixing the fences on the Penrice Estate and couldn't find another one. So we'd poached two pheasants, me and my brother, Dai. Yes, trapped them we did, and walked into Swansea to sell them. Took us twelve hours it did, and then we had the money robbed from us by a gang of louts from the Sandfields on the way home. I didn't want to go back to the house empty handed, because I was trying to be the man. So yes, I took the sheep . . . cut its throat and bled it so we'd have meat to eat and Mam wouldn't die too." The dark eyes filled and the voice faltered as he spoke.

"Then the Walkers came down from Scotland and set me up. The authorities put me on that hell boat. I never saw my family again – at least only when I could sleep and dream . . .

"But then we docked, and there was this girl, Beth, – part aborigine she was. Yes, with curly black hair and she laughed a lot. She saved me. She told me stories and helped take away the pain, and bit by bit, I tried to forget Horton and Mam and Dai and all the others, and I had to make my life again. If I didn't I'd have gone mad with worrying about them all. But I prayed every night that Jesus would take care of them."

95

Lizzie stared right through him, as if his words were etching themselves into her very soul. She, too, was reliving his former life.

"Yes," she went on. "That girl on the quayside when you docked, part aborigine was right, but only a quarter. My grandmother was a full aborigine from Queensland. It was quite a disgrace when she had Violet, my mother, with a white man. So she ran away south to New South Wales and worked in a saloon to raise her little girl, my mother, and try to send her to school. Then my mother became a servant in the Governor's house. She used to light the fires. She was the one who showed me how to roll the papers and fold the ends in, and then lay the sticks, not too many because she loved the trees, all criss-crossed and even. She married a man from Scotland, my father. They had me and my sister and brother, but I was the lightest one and they thought I was quite pretty with fair skin and dark eyes and hair . . . Yes, it was a lovely autumn day when the ship arrived and all the prisoners were herded off. I saw you at once – very skinny, bag of bones really, but there was something about you that attracted me, even then. After all that sailing your land legs wobbled and you fell flat on your face on the quay side. The sailors laughed at you and I did feel sorry."

"Yes, and you came up to me with a ladle of water from the bucket by the bollards . . . You saved me, Beth . . ."

A sudden wave crashed against the harbour wall, throwing its salt spray high into the air. Catapulted back into the present, Rob and Lizzie stared into one another's eyes, as if they were seeing for the first time. Rob's voice was hoarse.

"Did this really happen to us, Lizzie . . . or should I say 'Beth'?"

Lizzie simply threw back her tousled curls and her body shook as she laughed and cried with joy.

Frank Thomas

A SHORT CAT TAIL

I am known hereabouts as the Cat with the Black Whiskers. I realise that this sounds impressive, as if I were important, powerful and an object of fear. I am actually none of these things. Frankly, I am just a run-of-the-mill mouser.

I do not need to be important, powerful or frightening, for I am well served by two humans who pander to my every whim. Typical of their kind, they are incredibly capable of making, mending and inventing while being quite illogical in their way of life.

Humans have curious, pointless and repetitive rituals which occupy their waking lives. They constantly move things around unnecessarily; they call this "cleaning and tidying". They use tools called "cutlery" to eat from dishes which they then rub in hot water with a strange green fluid which they buy with their food from some place far away.

They constantly play with talking toys called TV sets, and talk to themselves whilst holding a thing against their ear. Some cut the fur off their faces every day, while others occasionally scrape it off their legs.

Instead of sleeping when they have nothing better to do, they sleep when it is dark, which is the best hunting time. They wear clothes, not to keep them warm but, apparently, to look different and not like humans at all. They even change their clothing to go to sleep!

I think probably the most foolish thing about people is their inability to live together in an ordered society with agreed rules of behaviour for the common good. They are all, to varying degrees, greedy, selfish, opinionated and stupid.

However, why should we cats complain? We are fed well by them and with a little applied psychology can easily persuade our carer slaves to provide extra delicacies to tempt us to eat! We are provided with milk, with warmth and with affectionate caresses.

I am personally extra fortunate in having a subsidiary human who lives in my territory and who obligingly goes out in the rain to let me into my home as and when required. This human has all the illogical habits of his kind except one – tidying! However, he has a redeeming willingness to tickle my tummy when I roll over to invite this liberty!

Occasionally, this same human harbours a large dog which seriously upsets the even tenor of our lives. Whilst this intruder is far from welcome, I have subdued his natural ebullience so that we co-exist, if not in amity, then in a state of armed neutrality.

My territory extends into the farmyard where I was born and I visit it daily to meet the calls of nature and to keep in touch with my less fortunate relatives, and cat world affairs.

I know that there are other chosen cats living in various surrounding habitations and I am considering organising a protest movement against a current invasion of refugee polecats and tame rabbits in the locality. A hunger strike would be ridiculous – a typical human stupidity – so I am going to suggest that we all insist on a diet of guinea fowl until our demands are met.

Linda Dobbs

CLOSE OBSERVATION OF A SPECIAL PLACE

I was inspired to write this by a visit to a Cadw Welsh Historic Monument – Castell Coch at Tongwynlais.

To quote the 1987 Cadw guidebook: Castell Coch is astonishing. It is a spectacular 'castle in the air' which was actually built; a pseudo-medieval stronghold made possible by the combination of the wealth and enthusiasm of a great patron, and the vision of his architect. As it stands, among beech woods on a steep hillside overlooking the valley of the River Taff, Castell Coch is one of the most romantic buildings in the British Isles. Commissioned by John Patrick Crichton Stuart, third Marquis of Bute in 1871, and designed by architect William 'Ugly' Burges (1827-1881), 'the structure seen today is the result of what a scholarly Victorian architect thought an original thirteenth century castle ought to look like'.

I chose to use a voice contemporary with the time of completion of the Castell, in 1891 . . .

Extract from the summer diary of
Gwendoline Howard Stuart, Lady Bute
July, 1891

Today, joy of joys, God rewarded us with His gift of splendid summer weather for the official handing over of the castle keys to my dear husband, whose lifetime passion is now complete. Patrick's pride and obvious contentment are overshadowed with great sorrow that 'Ugly' could not personally see this architectural triumph, in the shape of our immodestly resurrected Castell Coch.

Chapple & Frame have excelled themselves in their unfailing attention to fine detail, as Burges would have wished. Indeed, Ugly would have been overflowing with pride today, to stand within the walls of what has become, surely, his most romantic posthumous monument.

Excitement and enchantment surround me and beckon me on at every turn. There is an almost magical quality to the very stones and mortar, which has been bestowed by the sweeping away of the last vestiges of rubble and waste by the workmen and our servants. All is renewed. From out of the ancient citadel ashes has the awesome Phoenix arisen, which gives me such overwhelming pleasure and in which I already feel so at peace. Perhaps it is the progress of the past sixteen years which has comforted me so; watching the castle develop has required as much dedication by Patrick and William as Patrick and I have given to nurturing our family to their adolescences. I do hope they will feel as I do about Castell Coch.

Landscaping on the cleared hillside approach, south of the castle, moves on apace. Long after we have gone to dust will there be myriad oak, ash, sycamore and magnificent beeches to crown, green as emeralds, the stark and solid rock escarpment which towers above the Taff. The river sparkles below. I can see it clearly from the topmost turret window. This aspect pleases me and fills my senses. I can see forever. I flow with the current, seawards, in times of uninterrupted reverie.

Our carriage and four now has unrestricted access to the very drawbridge spanning the foundations-deep dry moat. I think of my approach today as perhaps an ancient yeoman would have done as he stormed the medieval walls. But I had none of his struggle and felt the immediacy of the sweetest sanctuary within the entrance gate. The courtyard is intimate and now vibrant with the rainbow colours of summer perennials in empty half-firkins, painted white to contrast with the steel-grey of the huge building blocks.

To stand in this sheltered 'O' of perfectly dressed limestone masonry is to wonder at Burges' vision and application in recreating the new from what remained of the ruins ravaged by six centuries of utter neglect. The product of his survey and invention rises all about me, protecting me, inviting me on to explore every curve of the curtain wall.

Today has been like a drawing room game on a massive scale, a game I want to play over and over again, so that I miss none of its enthralling intricacies as I make my moves on the board, my rank elevated now to Queen of the Castle in these majestic surroundings. My king has spared nothing from his counting-house to recreate this fantastic castle in the air!

Patrick has decided that we will reside here occasionally in the summer months and venture with the children to the Beacons and pretty Black Mountains east of the river. From the valley below, passers-by can watch our forest grow around the soaring conical towers, enveloping all who dwell within. In the far future, will they look upon our fortress as a fairytale dormitory, all within sleeping for one hundred years?

Patrick has plans to establish a vineyard. He will need an estate manager, of course, and some of the staff will come up from Cardiff. The children will be happiest with Emlyn and Gwynneth Thomas and their nephew Rhys, I'm sure, and Rhys has offered to teach the children some of the Welsh language – certainly its pronunciation – but will they sit still long enough to absorb what he has to say? Surely, if they retire to the drawing room here they will find inspiration enough for serious chatter and study? Or will they be distracted by the exuberant splendour of the décor in this inspired, vaulted space?

They are likely to enjoy the lively scenes of animals, birds, butterflies and stars suspended above them between the vaulted ribs and falling to the upper gallery level. My neck and shoulders ache so when I study these closely.

Later, we can explain to the children the themes of Life and Death in Nature, which are all around. The lower wall murals contain 58 different flower patterns. I will set the children a long holiday task to record all they see in this ornamental sanctum of the Keep Tower.

Dare I confide in this journal the exquisite sensual delight I try hard to conceal from the children, as I enter my very own turret bedchamber? Shall I sense the timelessness of the slumber of a sleeping beauty high in the Keep Tower? Will Patrick be my prince, fighting back the entwined bramble and thorn canopy, to awaken me each new day, bestowing his eager kisses on my parted, pale rose lips?

No labour has been spared to enchant the eye here. The Moorish arches to the circular walls of my nest, high above what will become the lush tree canopy, are supported by carved gold-encrusted branches. I will sleep tonight on a scarlet and gold bed adorned with eight perfect clear crystal spheres which will reflect the candle light from sconces and send our writhing shadows to chase the uppermost recesses of the domed space above. Our lovemaking suspended above us, an animated etching in the mirrored glass panels, will be the perfect counterpane coverlet to draw over this fine day.

I will never allow the children access beyond the spiral stair passageway leading upwards from my Lord's quarters. This, my haven and heavenly safe place, will be where I will worship my Lord's enterprise and where he will find unending adoration from his most loyal subject.

I dream! No, this is reality about me and how blessed and fortunate I am. It is time for us all to gather together below to celebrate this most wondrous work of art. My pen must await the morrow.

I wonder: how large a set of keys is needed to secure Castell Coch?

- -

Reni Stableforth

THE SCULPTOR
(for Peter Nicholas)

He moulds his clay with grey-slicked hands,
Slides his palms over the shape he has created.
Waiting, as his caked hands dry,
His eyes carve the dancer.

He takes his knife, delicately nicks
The blind eye sockets,
Opens a mouth, folds back a finger,
Tweaks toes into pas-de-deux stance.

The figure now lives,
Dances before him on one foot,
Pegged to the earth.

Barbara Griffiths

CHRISTMAS MUSINGS

Just me talking to myself . . .

Come on, you can do it – just write a Christmas story – you've rattled things off in the past – why can't you do it now?

Come on – get a glass of sherry and a mince pie and sit down at the computer – ideas will come, everyone says that – the ideas will just come.

Come on, as it's Christmas it is a *bit* special – all the group will have made an effort.

Frank will have written another original and unusual tale.

Mike will produce a poem with flowing words about the sea on Christmas day.

David will have written another really funny account about the children.

Margaret will have a splendid contribution – I'm sure.

Reni and Linda will produce wonderful, meaningful Christmas stories full of big words that I will try to remember and look up at home.

Vernon will have a funny little item to tell with a twist.

And then there's Pam – what will she produce this time? It will be hard for her to do anything better than **Not Pam, One Hand Clap** – and **No Sound Tree Falling** – will it be 'No Turkey Cooking'! – or – 'No Santa if no Chimney'!

Anyway, Barb – just think of something – think of your own Christmases past and see if one of them will spark off your imagination.

What about just after the war when the family had a parcel from America with a whole chicken in a tin, salted peanuts and a tin of peaches? – that was special.

Or – your first Christmas in Africa? – sweltering under a tin-roofed veranda, eating a turkey dinner in the sunshine – that was different.

Then there was the time, newly married in Zimbabwe, when we both accepted separate invitations for Christmas dinner – one was at lunch time and one was in the evening – we were so full yet it was fun.

Then, the Christmas Sian was born – and we took her to Midnight mass in Bulawayo. Her cries echoed through the cathedral – unforgettable.

What about taking your first grandchild, dressed as a shepherd, to church in Swansea? – when he just casually marched up the aisle, took the baby Jesus from the crib, cradled him in his arms and sat contentedly by the priest on the altar steps for the rest of the service.

Not one of the Gospels has that version of the story.

They are all wonderful memories. Don't they give you ideas?

No – not really.

Well – what about Horton? – that's been great, hasn't it? Last year was your first here and you've had such a wonderful time.

Making a grotto for two grandsons in the garage.

The village carol singers came – and had mulled wine in Great House Court.

The grandchildren wrote their letters to Santa – and Owain wanted his letter to say 'Any nice toy – no nasty stuff please.'

A lovely Christmas morning service in Llandewi Church – with the animals in the fields outside.

The whole family had a walk on Horton beach.

Our Boxing Day picnic at Mewslade – just magic.

Ok, Barb, give in – your imagination has failed you – you haven't got a story – but you relished going over those memories.

Think of this year now. What have you got in mind? What will you hope for? Don't worry about being corny or sentimental.

Well here is the truth –

Sorry – no story.

But, I can't imagine or want to be anywhere else other than where I am now – waiting for another Christmas in this lovely, funny, crazy-at-times village.

Reni Stableforth

BEHIND CLOSED LIDS

I cannot . . . cannot find the words
to rip open rage,
and if so exposed,
how could I bring to bear
my anger . . . my grief?

Who would sense the sting,
yield to my roaring wrath . . .
Can a branch riven by nature's storm
parry the blame
or cry in sorrow?

My child was hurled up . . .
Left ravaged like a broken doll,
his perfection bled
and drained of strong limbs.

Like a callow candle flame is capped
so youth was swiftly spent
with neck-splintering bone, his childhood
leftover hurricane sweepings.

Would only that his wounds, and mine,
could heal as swiftly
with these written words
unleashed.

Yet, always . . . though my eyes
caress his stilled strength
. . . he will run
behind closed lids.

Vernon Griffiths

THE LOCKET

Harry Trencher had never had it so good. Not for a long time, anyway. There had been occasions in the past when he had been lucky enough to find a coin or two in the gutter, usually more of the bronze kind than silver, but this was his very special day.

The locket had caught his eye where it lay, gleaming golden-bright, half hidden in a motley pile of autumn leaves. He stooped and breathed an instant sigh of relief, for there was no one in sight. With one swift movement, born of experience, he deftly pocketed his find and continued to saunter along as if he hadn't a care in the world. And, why *should* he worry? His newly acquired possession was as good as cash in hand. If his memory could be relied upon, just around the corner was a guaranteed buyer. Trencher would not haggle or quibble today – he was that desperate.

Coming back to his home town made him think, once again, of those happier times when he had a family to care for; a lovely young daughter and a wife he adored. To him it had been an idyllic world – a world shattered when another man appeared on the scene. What made it so much worse was that the other man was no stranger. Trencher had always been too busy working to realise the significance of the man's constant presence in his home. When the parting from his family came for him, it was abrupt and very painful. In despair, he had taken to the streets. He had no home; he had nothing to call his own. He didn't belong anywhere.

Trencher was stung back to reality when he saw the three balls of the pawnbroker sign and realised that his memory had served him well. Pausing for a moment to study his reflection in the window, he saw what he had become – a dirty, dishevelled wreck of a man. His clothes were tattered and torn and his face was hidden in an under-growth of beard. The only thing that cheered him was the name he had assumed. He had chosen 'Trencher' because he liked its ring.

First, he checked to make sure the locket was safe before going into the premises, then, he braced himself for the inevitable head-on collision with 'Jack-the-Balls' inside. They were all 'Jack-the-Balls' to him. He despised each and every one of them. He didn't put up much of a fight, as he wasn't in the mood, so he got less than the locket was worth. But, he took the ready cash as though it were a gift from the gods. Stepping out into the street, he made for the nearest pub, but, before he could go inside to spend his profit from the deal, he felt an unfriendly grip on his shoulder.

"Not so fast, old man. You are under arrest!"

Trencher's recollection of the incident was hazy. He doubted whether he had been advised of his rights, and he guessed he'd been shopped. The events that followed his arrest went too quickly for him to grasp, but, whatever they were, he found himself in a cell. This was the first time this had happened to him and he felt humiliated.

Coming before the magistrates added to his indignity. Their contempt for a vagrant was blatantly obvious. The chief magistrate even had the gall to slip in a lecture before remanding him for a week.

The charge was one of theft and nobody bothered to listen to his story.

"I didn't steal it, I didn't steal it," shouted Trencher, protesting his innocence. "I picked the bloody thing up from the gutter!"

His pleas were ignored and back to the cell he went.

During the next few days, it dawned on Trencher that he was becoming a pawn in some game. The locket was obviously worrying the police as they kept on asking him how he had come to have it in his possession – and what else did he have squirreled away. They tried very hard to force a confession from him but, when that didn't work, he was advised he needed someone to represent him. It was that serious.

Eventually, his appointed solicitor had the courtesy to inform him that he, Trencher, had handled stolen property – part of a haul from a recent burglary. To make matters worse, the locket had been torn from the neck of its owner as she lay asleep – and when she was woken by this sudden violence she had been further assaulted.

Trencher was horrified. "How could anyone think I could commit such a crime?"

"I think quite a few people would be persuaded to believe it – given your demeanour and appearance," replied the solicitor. "But we can do something about your appearance at least."

The description given by the victim fitted Trencher's build and age, even down to the beard – and, even more damning, the distraught young woman had picked him out at the identity parade.

But, in court at the end of the week, it was a different matter when she saw Trencher spruced up and clean-shaven.

"No, that's not the man!" she cried. "It's definitely not him!"

Amidst the legal confusion, the major charge of aggravated theft was dropped. However, the opportunity to lecture Trencher again was not lost. He was warned of the consequence of handling stolen property and then bound over to be on his best behaviour.

If only Harry Trencher could have spoken to the lady of the locket, then perhaps he would have had some cause to reflect. He wasn't to know that she had stood up for him in court because he reminded her of her own father – a father who had long ago disappeared and left no trace. In her eyes, Trencher was what her father might have become.

As Trencher made to leave the courthouse, half dazed by the turn of events, he was jostled several times. But it wasn't until he was outside that he felt around his pockets, more or less out of habit. To his surprise, he discovered a bulging envelope almost falling out of one of them. He looked around, mindful of what the judge had so recently said to him, but apart from a lady in a large blue hat and, he thought, the young woman from the witness box, there was no one hanging around. The two women got into a car before he could reach them and were driven away.

On the edge of the pavement he examined the package – inside it were twenty five-pound notes! He counted them again and again. Bewildered and very misty eyed he shuffled across the road.

He didn't see the car that struck and flung him into the air.

He didn't see the ambulance that arrived too late to save him.

When Harry Trencher's body was lifted onto a stretcher, a tiny piece of court notepaper fluttered from a pocket. Its message was simple.

'To my love – I'm sorry'.

Linda Dobbs

CONVERSATION AT A WEDDING

You meet folks like her at the annual company dinner and dance. They slide up to you, ingratiating themselves firmly into your space, widen their eyes – by hoisting their eyebrows – and bore through you with the inevitable interrogative drill.

"And what connection do you have with so and so?" they begin, mainly out of nosiness; sometimes because no-one else, all evening, has been interested enough in them to pose the same question.

And so it was with Mrs Hunter senior. She kept an eagle eye on the guests all through the wedding breakfast and, following one or two longer, inquisitive – or were they purposeful? – glances at me, and the obviously forced enquiry of her immediate neighbour at the top table, she graciously excused herself and moved crabwise, past Mr Grant, and along towards the powder room, smoothing the creases in her over-tight, silk skirt as she moved. Now the guests could relax after the formality of the speeches. The jazz quartet started to tune up for the post-feasting stomp.

It had been a quiet day for me, so far. I spoke only when spoken to. I only wanted to watch; not be a part of any of the happiness and satisfaction that was obviously felt by everyone on the top table. Colin had eyes for Jilly only, that much was certain. I found it hard to accept, and my heart went out to the new, junior, Mrs Hunter. She did look exquisite and, judging by the condition of Colin's new mother-in-law, Jilly Grant would wear well for him. Perhaps Colin's decision had been partly based on the time-honoured recommendation to look at a prospective wife's mother to see how she has worn over the years.

"Doesn't Jilly look stunning, and so like her mother, don't you think?" came the appraising tone at my ear level, as Colin's mother slipped into the empty seat beside me.

"The blush of silk and the blooms in her bouquet give her skin the same look of velvety peaches and cream, and isn't it wonderful how all the guests have somehow, magically, managed to blend in with the bride's chosen colour scheme? My dear you, too, look radiant! The magenta is so dramatic . . . are you a friend of Jilly's?" she enquired, and I felt instantly uncomfortable, as I struggled to gain some composure. I'd not expected to have to say more than 'how do you do?' or 'how interesting' all the day long. I only wanted to be there to watch. Colin said he wanted me to watch and listen to everything carefully, so that I would know for certain.

"Yes, yes, I'm Jilly's third year Swansea room-mate and I wouldn't have missed this for the world." I lied, summoning up my cheeriest of sideways grins, as I took in Mrs Hunter's veiled features almost on a level with my shoulder. "I think Colin's a very lucky chap to have such a beautiful wife," I offered. I meant it. Jilly was gorgeous.

"I can tell you, it's more than I'd ever hoped for," confided Colin's mother. "He's such a catch for any girl and I thought he'd never settle down. But Jilly's certainly worked some charm. They're obviously very much in love. Isn't that nice in this day and age?" and she shifted her ample bottom, smoothed her skirt down her fat thighs once more and settled back for what promised to be an eternity. I wondered if she danced. If Jilly and Colin led the dancing, would Mr Grant rescue me from my ambush, by accompanying my inquisitor onto the floor? I prayed the jazz band would soon be in tune.

"Yes, I agree with you. One can drift into and out of so many promising situations. But I suppose when love really comes along, you know it'll be for ever. Let's hope Jilly and Colin live happily together for ever after . . ." I recited, slightly maudlin now and self-pitying.

It should have been me, you know. I almost whispered out loud. But I just continued to watch, my eyes pricking now with the permeating haze issuing from several cigar-smoking guests.

Mrs Hunter continued. "What I find so rewarding about today is that I feel Colin's going to the very best hands, after mine of course. I really feel that she'll look after him better than many a lass we've heard about in the past. I suppose you won't know too much about my Colin, as you're a friend of the bride, but it's been quite a challenge keeping up with all his women. At any rate, Jilly's aware of his previous shortcomings. She'll guide him. They'll be good together, don't you think?"

"I'm sure that as they've made their vows today, it has to be right," I said, though why I chose this reasoning was instantly beyond me. Colin had wanted to exchange vows with me not fourteen months earlier, but I'd been cautious, wondering how I'd ever be able 'to have and to hold' this outrageous charmer of a man. I lost my opportunity. Along came Jilly, and any female who had ever known, adored, loved or bedded Colin stood never another chance. He had eyes only for her.

"It was a lovely ceremony. I was so pleased the tiny bridesmaids behaved. Did Jilly not ask you to be her maid of honour, or should I say matron? I see you are married, but I sense you're all alone here as Jilly's guest," Mrs Hunter persisted.

Oh, why don't you go away and leave me here to watch, you nosey, brassy, overblown cow, I screamed inside. I looked down at the bright gold band on my left hand.

"Yes, you're right. I'm married, but widowed by a golfing tournament this weekend!" I chuckled breezily, and continued – going for the kill now – "just as well, really, otherwise the situation might have developed awkwardly today. You see, my man is one of Jilly's ex-lovers and I'd not have wanted him pining after an old flame, particularly on her wedding day."

Triumphant now, I turned my cheeky raised brows and wide grin to gloat over Mrs Hunter's expression and possible disquiet. But her face remained quite bland, calm, collected.

She patted my right hand intimately. "Well, it's been very nice meeting you my dear, I'm sure," she breathed, as she slowly rose from the chair, quite obviously burning to say something more. "I think you're very wise to have come along on your own today. It wouldn't do to have too many ex-lovers on the scene, especially on such an important day for these two. You know what I mean, don't you?" She brushed her palm lightly across my shoulder and glided away to chat once more with the bride's parents. I continued to watch, in stunned silence . . .

Frank Thomas

CITY LIFE

When I was very young, I used to visit London fairly frequently. I stayed with a favourite uncle and aunt and was treated like a visiting prince.

All the wonderful sights of the city were opened to me – the Houses of Parliament, Madame Tussauds, The Tower of London, Gamages Toy Shop, the Zoo, The Palace, the Serpentine. I was bedazzled by the endless experience presented for my pleasure and interest. The place itself, the homes and small shops and daily life appeared to me to be just like my home town, only on a rather greater scale.

It seems to me that the attraction exerted by city life on children and young people generally is the excitement of the place. Something is always happening – boredom appeared unthinkable. The concentration of people and money means that all things are viable and available, whether one's desires are entertainment, exotic food, artistic events, vice, spectacle, crime or big money making. If one lives in the country or even a small town, then it appears that all the desirable things in one's young life are lacking for one reason or another and can only be available in cities!

I have never been to Pompeii but have read about its fate. I have, though, been in London and other cities and watched beautiful buildings, people's homes and public utilities collapsing in flames and in chaos. I have watched on television the complete destruction of Grozny by Russian troops. One cannot witness or experience such calamitous events without becoming aware of the fragility of these anthills teeming with human life, throbbing with the movement and energy of mankind's power, invention and restless activity.

Last summer, I drove through Rotterdam's port complex to board the Channel ferry to Harwich. All through the maze of roads, warehouses, pylons, cranes, transformers, utilities and other man-made jigsaws I wonder how any local or port authority could possibly monitor the activity and expansion of all this human activity. The supply and consumption of electricity and water, the proper disposal of human and industrial waste, the safety of industrial workers, the control of development, the policing of crime – in a city of which this immense area is only a part – how much more can it develop before it is ripe for a major disaster?

Have you ever, when gardening, put a spade into an anthill and then watched the occupants of the ant-city scurry about here and there, not knowing where to go, moving their precious eggs from danger to anywhere so long as it is away from the disaster area? That is the way we humans have no alternative but to behave when a city is suddenly subject to catastrophe.

It is hard enough to cope when rivers flood unexpectedly and submerge carpets, furniture, food and toys in a sudden, stinking mess, but at least there is usually, in such areas of low population density, a means of escape, a rescue service of sorts and an uncomfortable return to normality in due course. Destruction of a city, either by bombing or prolonged breakdown of power, water, and communication, is almost too cataclysmic to contemplate: children and elderly people isolated in lifts or skyscraper flats, superstores emptied of provisions, looters hell-bent on survival, death and disease suddenly at close quarters.

Rural life may not be exciting but suddenly seems much more attractive.

Barbara Griffiths

THOUGHTS AT ABERGLASNEY

Alone and peaceful,
Surrounded by beauty
My mind is at ease,
I'm happy and calm.
Tangled thoughts push in,
And aim to disturb me.
I must forget them,
There's no cause for alarm.

A whole day for me
Was the plan of it all,
To sketch or write
Among the trees so tall.
But invasive as ever,
Worries probe and prod.
Please leave me alone
In this garden with God.

At this stage in life
My course is all set.
Retirement is fine,
No problems as yet.
But when major cares
Go out through the door,
In come the small ones,
Just more and more.

Great minds are deep,
As deep as the sea.
Mine is brimful of trivia
"Oh dear – what's for Tea?"

David Griffiths

PLAYMATES

They pranced and played around her legs and feet. Over the past weeks the little girl had come to know them well and they became her friends. She especially loved the little ones and the way they tickled her toes. Day after day on the sand, like spring lambs, they gambolled and frolicked together. There was no need to say much as, with shrieks of laughter, they enjoyed their games of run and catch.

As each day dawned, as soon as she could, she eagerly made her way over the low grassy dunes to look for her playmates. She always found them waiting for her to join them and begin the dance of their carefree hours together.

She had wondered if she would be lonely here, far from home, but on her first visit to the beach she had found all the company she needed. From the moment they came together she had loved being with these lively companions.

Now, the summer holiday was coming to an end and she was with them for the last time. They had a very happy day – full of fun and daring antics, but when she told them that today she was leaving them they surged around her. As they gently held her close their large warm tears splashed down on her feet.

She tore herself away, made her way up the beach and turned to wave her final goodbye.

Would they miss her? Would they remember her? Would they make new friends?

She gazed back for a while – then smiled, glad to see that already they were playing games with another child.

She raised both hands and saw them reply with white foamy fingers on hands of spray held high by the arms of young waves.

Pamela El-Hosaini

THE ABSOLUTE

Softly You call to me, but engrossed in trivia
I am too busy to hear.
Patiently You wait.

With gentle persistence You are ever close,
But I am untouched by Your presence.
Patiently You wait.

In moments of solitude I sense You beckon,
My soul feels Your healing touch.
But worldly cares carry me away.

You bring joy, yet in the midst of it I stray.
But when pain and despair carve out their chasm
I selfishly reach out for You.

I need You in serenity, not only times of torment.
But if sadness draws me close
Then let the chasm be endless.

Let me reach Your peace, and let Us share the bliss
And awe of knowing We are one,
That I am whole, complete.

In silent meditation I feel Your warm glow within,
While moments of tranquillity
Whisper all is well.

My eyes see and ears hear what my heart has always known.
I surrender to the love
That keeps me in Your embrace.

Our boundless spirit, united within, fills creation,
And I remember in humility that
Patiently You wait.

For when You hold me near, despair and sorrow melt away,
Ecstasy wells up inside
And I rest in the heart of God.

Linda Dobbs

FLOOD ON THE SOUTH GOWER ROAD

Persistent raindrops pond in a hollow
where drakes and ducks,
quick to seize dabbling opportunities,
materialise to wallow
in this chance habitat.

Webbed feet wade in,
to paddle serenely in the swirling maelstrom
of surface torrent from the Bryn.
The feathered raft
shows no trepidation.

Nor bedraggled bovine,
hind-quarters windward,
mouths grazing ground
standing proud of the flood.
They continue a-munching then chewing the cud.

Frank Thomas

A RURAL TALE

David was a third generation farmer – proud, hard working, independent and good-humoured – but not an ideal man to cross.

His pet hates were 'jacks-in-office' – people who revelled in exercising power by virtue of their jobs. This antipathy undoubtedly stemmed from his childhood, when he often watched his tenant farmer father being treated as if he was a serf by the estate's agent. One of the happiest days of David's life came when the estate was broken up and he was able to buy the farm and be his own master.

Some time later, David leased a small plot of land on the edge of his farm to his bank manager who wanted to build a bungalow for his retirement. Planning regulations were non-existent at that time and David had had in mind building another house on his land for his own use when his young son, William, eventually took over the farm. Having somebody else build the house was an ideal solution for him.

However, long before David was due to retire, both the bank manager and his wife died and the bungalow was put up for sale.

The new owners seemed pleasantly friendly, but hailed from an urban background. They found the innate curiosity and interest of the villagers intrusive and had obvious difficulty in dealing with the fine nuances of social grading and relationships in village life. The dustmen, the postman, the mobile butcher, the village shopkeeper, the villagers who lit bonfires, the dog owners, the horse riders, the village children and everybody else who came into contact with them became aware of the newcomers' views on village life. In short – they were unpopular.

Breaking point was reached when an environmental health inspector visited the farm. He came to investigate a complaint, by the bungalow owners, about the dreadful smells generated by the farm activities.

The inspector was, actually, very understanding and appreciative of the farmer's problem. He was a level-headed, knowledgeable young man who knew all about slurry pits, silage and muck-spreading. He said that he found the farm atmosphere rather refreshing and certainly more attractive than some areas of town on a Sunday morning. The inspector departed saying he would do his best to placate the complainants.

Unfortunately, the inspector's best efforts were obviously not good enough and relations between the parties continued to deteriorate.

One Saturday evening, in the local pub, an impromptu 'council of war' took place, led by David and attended by the postman, the butcher, the baker and anyone else who cared to join in. The village constable, an ex-navy man, gave the discussion a new sense of direction. He had served in the Far East and various hot spots when Great Britain still ran an empire and half the world was still coloured red on the map.

"In the good old days," he said, "when the diplomats failed and we had to settle local troubles, we used to send a gunboat up the Yangtse River, or into the port or wherever, just to underline the possibilities if the nonsense continued. It usually worked very well. 'Gunboat Diplomacy' the Liberals used to call it!"

A smile began to emerge on David's face and after a few more rounds of ale, everybody went home refreshed, primed and determined.

The following week the bungalow's dustbin was upset, either by foxes or village dogs, and the contents were strewn everywhere. Several mornings saw late postal deliveries to the newcomers and, one day, the mail was soaking wet through being caught in the floods.

A blackbird family began to target certain milk bottle caps in search of cream – and local garden bonfires seemed to burn for ever. Delivery of the *Radio Times* and *The Guardian* became erratic and the baker frequently ran out of sliced wholemeal loaves before reaching the bungalow. Horse droppings and dog dirt in the vicinity of the bungalow increased, as if by magic, and the cockerel in a neighbour's garden not only arose earlier, but also crowed louder than before.

When David spent two days muck-spreading near the bungalow, the unhappy residents decided that rural life was not for them. They departed – putting the bungalow up for sale. This time, David bought it in readiness for his own retirement.

When David did retire, no-one, except the dustman, the postman, the baker, the village policeman and a few other locals could understand how anybody could give their house such an odd name as 'Gumboot Diplomacy'.

Tarrick El-Hosaini

HOW LONG IS A PIECE OF STRING?

Have you ever held a string,
Or pulled it taut – and heard it sing
When softly plucked by fingertips,
Or strummed or teased with fiddling sticks?

Have you fixed a washing line
To peg a sodden week's design
And had it sag – or just give way,
So all its cargo's mud and clay?

Have you skipped in skittish school
Or pranced to flirt, or played the fool
To tempt your kit with tangled yarn
And end in Gordian knots? – gosh darn!

Have you seen a dangling noose
Or hanging, cut your best mate loose,
And used the rope to tow his car
And inched along but never get far?

Have you roped a bucking steed
And broke her in, then felt the need
To tether a mad bull by lasso
And taste his 'rocky oysters' too?

Have you laced your gyms in bows
But split the things and stubbed your toes,
Or can't afford a plaster first,
Then wonder why your blister's burst?

So if you've tried what's spelled before
Or seen or heard it mentioned more,
Just think upon this simple thing:
There's more than ends to every string.

Editors:
Margaret Rees
Reni Stableforth

Enquiries about
The Horton Writing Group
To
01792 391356

Summer 2003

Price: £4.00

Cover illustration from an original watercolour
by Frank Thomas

Printed in Wales by Dinefwr Press, Llandybie, Carmarthenshire, SA18 3YD